Healing with
Mind Power

HEALING
WITH
MIND
POWER

Richard Shames, M.D. and
Chuck Sterin, M.S., M.F.C.C.

Rodale Press • Emmaus, Pa.

4   6   8   10   9   7   5   3

Library of Congress Cataloging in Publication Data

Shames, Richard.
  Healing with mind power.

  Includes index.
  1. Autogenic training. I. Sterin, Chuck, joint author. II. Title.
RC499.A8S52   615'.8512   78-4551
ISBN 0-87857-210-4

*Rich dedicates this book to his family,
the best single group of teachers anywhere.
Chuck dedicates this book to Joan,
his wife and best friend.*

Contents

ACKNOWLEDGMENTS   ix

PART I: THEORY

   1. What Is Self-Hypnosis?   3
   2. Hypnosis and Suggestion in Daily Life   11
   3. How Hypnosis Got Started and Became Accepted   19

PART II: TECHNIQUE

   4. How to Do It   29
   5. Helpful Hints and Reassurance   48

PART III: EVERYDAY PRACTICAL USES

   6. Stress Reduction, Relaxation, and Inner Peace   57
   7. Changing Harmful Habits   73
   8. Self-Hypnosis for Self-Healing   89
   9. Exploring Extra-ordinary States   100

PART IV: A KEY TOOL FOR TOTAL HEALTH

   10. Waking Up to Ourselves   113
   11. Putting Ourselves in Our Own Hands   125
   12. Enjoying the Holistic Lifestyle   136

ADDENDUM: A MANUAL FOR WHOLENESS   149

INDEX   177

Acknowledgments

Acknowledgment is hereby given by Chuck to the Portland Academy of Hypnosis, and by Rich to Martin Orne, hypnosis professor at the University of Pennsylvania Medical School, for their keen inspiration and warm encouragement. We also gratefully acknowledge our talented friend Don Rosenthal for his invaluable editorial contributions, as well as Ruth Halley for so skillfully typing the manuscript.

I

Theory

I

What Is Self-Hypnosis?

We would like to share with you in the following pages what could be the most powerful tool that medical science has at its disposal. It is also one that each of us has readily available for our own use. It has gone by many names down through the years, including a variety of religious names. Some have called it the power of suggestion. Others have called it mind control. Still others have called it meditation. Many doctors and psychiatrists, and now the lay public, call it self-hypnosis.

Almost every culture has in its own way stumbled upon this tool by exploring deeper layers of consciousness. Each culture has explained these extra-ordinary states in accordance with its own beliefs, and has surrounded its discoveries with its own names and structures. But underneath the different words remains a strong thread of similarity, a general idea which keeps reoccurring throughout history: there are states of consciousness different from both ordinary waking and sleeping. These less common states combine aspects of both waking and sleeping in unique and potentially valuable ways. The "alpha" state, recently investigated with great intensity, is a good example.

With the invention of machines that measure the changing electrical patterns of the brain, it was found that certain states of mind correspond to certain measurable patterns on the machine. One pattern, which was named "alpha," was found to correspond quite closely to a state of mind in which the normal agitation was largely missing. When a person registers alpha waves on the machine the mind is both alert and very relaxed. The normal inner chatter of the waking mind is temporarily quiet; there is less stress and greater sensitivity. It is as if the more destructive aspects of the mind have gone to sleep, leaving the creative aspects to flourish unimpeded.

The *name* of this state, or the exact nature of its brain waves, is not what is important for us. What is important is to realize the tremendous power and potential in this blend of alertness and relaxation. It is in fact far more pregnant with possibilities than we may realize. In such a state we can have surprising control over our mental functioning for jobs like memory recall or problem solving. In addition, we can have increasing power over our physical being. Self-diagnosis, self-healing, and habit modification are all within our grasp.

To be more specific, we might want to increase our production of a certain hormone, or control our blood pressure, or lessen the tension in particular muscles. We can make our heart beat faster or slower and decrease the fluttering. We can cure our migraines. We can control the part of the brain called the reticular activating system, which has to do with sleeping and wakefulness. We can learn to modify our disposition and mood. In short, we can gain more control over what has been called our mind-body integration.

In doing this we are beginning to play with some powerful energies and to control them without fully understanding how they work, which is not unusual in science. In fact, it is possible that we are tapping into energies much more forceful and far-reaching than just our own being; we may be harnessing the forces of what Carl Jung called the Collective Unconscious.

The power of this technique has been dramatically demonstrated by people in dire need, people who are very strongly motivated. If you are applying the technique for something where there is little motivation involved, it's not likely to work as well as if the motivation is there and urgent. For example, a young man who was learning meditation and hypnosis was called into the military during the Viet Nam War. He was injured in combat and found himself alone, with a severed artery; he was unable to move or to do anything about it. He remembered his course in meditation and hypnosis, and realized that if ever he needed something urgently, it was now. So he employed the self-hypnotic techniques he'd learned, exercising his mental control to clamp down on the artery and stop the spurting of blood. This is normally unheard of; external pressure and immediate medical attention are considered indispensable for a severed artery. Hence the astonishment of the medic when he arrived to find the soldier comfortable, relaxed, and out of danger. From one perspective this was a miracle; from another, it was a most natural event.

There have been other stories like this, of superhuman feats that have occurred when the necessity was there. You may have heard about the woman who lifted up a car to save her baby from being crushed, or the man who stayed alive in an airtight bank vault by meditating and thereby slowing his respiration.

Doctors have known for a long time that some sick people can harness a great deal of energy to get better, and that others, less ill, get worse and die. They've called this energy the "will to live," the will to be healed. They sometimes notice what are called spontaneous recoveries from very advanced diseases. An example is when the doctor says, "I'm sorry to have to tell you this, but you have a terminal illness." And the patient says, "Hell, no, I'm going to beat this," and he does. And then later the doctor says, "Fantastic! You've had a spontaneous remission."

Well, that spontaneous remission may not have been so spontaneous. It may have been related to the consciousness and psychology of the person who was cured. The medical literature, the psychic literature, and the psychological literature are filled with research studies, anecdotal evidence, and stories about similar cases, all of which seem to employ one common, fundamental technique, which involves four basic ingredients.

What, then, are the ingredients of hypnosis? We just mentioned *motivation*, which may well be the most important ingredient. Take, for example, a pregnant woman in great pain with a difficult labor who lives way out in the country where there are no anesthetics or medicines. Suppose a hypnosis practitioner comes in and says, "I can help you with this. Do you want me to?" And the woman says, "Yes, yes, I do, I really do!" That woman goes into hypnosis very easily. Why? She very badly wants it to work. *A person who's got something that he or she really wants to do with hypnosis tends to get the desired results.* On the other hand, someone who isn't interested in being hypnotized or who doesn't have any particular reason to use hypnosis is usually difficult to hypnotize. So motivation, although not necessarily this extreme, is probably the major factor.

Another factor is *relaxation*. For hypnosis to happen there seems to be a need for at least a little relaxation at the beginning. Once you achieve this state, further relaxation comes more easily. The challenge for many people lies in attaining this initial relaxation. Allowing yourself the time or the space to do nothing else but be relaxed may be a prerequisite. That means actually giving yourself the space to say, "Okay, for these next ten minutes I'll put away everything else. I'm taking the telephone off the hook and arranging things so I won't be disturbed. I'm not going to concern myself with any other errands or business." Then there's a chance for some relaxation; you've arranged things in your favor.

You may also want to try manipulating the environment a little. Limiting some of the input is a way of giving yourself more "inner space," and you can do this in a variety of ways. You can close your eyes to limit visual input; many of the schools of meditation or hypnosis recommend just that. Visual activity in humans is a major part of brain function, so limiting that activity immediately helps to create more inner space, and makes it easier to relax.

Next, you may want to limit the other four senses if possible. Eliminating obvious distractions such as TV and records will help. You might also want to turn off hearing. We don't have "earlids" the same way we have eyelids, but we can relate differently to the sounds that are there by withdrawing our attention from them. We can notice the sounds without attending to them, without putting any energy into naming them, or commenting inwardly about them. Then the sounds are just part of the overall flow of events. They lose importance and are no longer a "distraction." In fact, there is now no longer any "distraction"—just the simple flow of events, which includes sound, smell, touch, breathing, thoughts, desires—everything that's taking place. To be in that kind of relationship to the flow of events brings an inner quietness without effort, the beginning of real relaxation.

The third ingredient of hypnosis is *concentration*. You will want to limit the things that you're working on to just one thing at a time. This might be likened to a lens that gathers the light of the sun and focuses it down to a single point. Just as the diffused energy of the sun can be focused into a single point and have tremendous power, so too can mental energy be focused. Generally we are accustomed to thinking and behaving in a rather scattered fashion. Sometimes we try to do three things at once, ending up without accomplishing anything well. We are used to being pulled in many different directions at the same time. Maybe this is why we are not as effective and efficient as we'd like to be.

On the other hand, by focusing on just one thing at a time you can concentrate your efforts and energies the same way a lens concentrates the diffused rays of the sun. Recall how as a child you were able to burn a hole through a piece of paper with a magnifying glass. Learning to focus mental energy similarly is one of the very common activities at many meditation centers. You can focus on a candle burning, on your own breathing, on sound, on a mantra, on any number of things both in the external and the internal worlds. Focusing on a mental picture, an image in the mind's eye, can be quite powerful. Self-hypnosis offers us this kind of concentrated energy which we can then apply towards self-healing, self-diagnosis, higher states of wellness, or greater levels of consciousness.

This brings us now to the fourth ingredient, which we'll call *directing*. Once you've achieved the motivation, once you've relaxed a bit, once you are in focus, then you can *apply* this technique by beginning to direct your energies. Directing energy is the crucial last step. It is here that we harness the energy for a specific purpose. The method is simply to *visualize* the desired result.

The use of visual directing is a common factor in many of these techniques. They call for imagining the part of the body you want healed, picturing it visually, and having it appear to get better. Some of the behavior modification techniques involve seeing a picture of yourself acting differently. If you vividly picture yourself behaving in a different way, the actual behavior often follows.

This visual component, or "visualization," is associated with all four ingredients of self-hypnosis. It may help you get motivated, relaxed, and focused. But visualization very definitely has tremendous importance for the fourth ingredient, directing the energy. As an analogy, any of the buildings we see around us existed first in the mind of the architect. First they were visualized, then put on paper, and finally the image became wood and concrete and steel.

Visualization is a tremendous aid in creating new patterns of behavior as well as new structures. We don't really know how it works, but there's something about it that does work amazingly well. People have cured themselves of malignant tumors by visualizing the blood cells of their immune system going in and gobbling up the cancer. When they are good at visualizing this and very positive about it, excellent results are common. Those who have trouble visualizing don't have the same success in self-healing. There have been people with diabetes who were told to visualize the pancreas working more effectively, secreting more insulin. It often worked for them if they were able to visualize it, see it with their imagination. There have been alcoholics who were trained in this technique and told to visualize themselves not taking that first drink, whether things were going well or badly. And the ones who could do this have had a high rate of sobriety.

It has been said that what exists inside is what comes to exist outside. People who go around always consumed with unhappy thoughts and negative mental visualizations tend to have their pictures eventually verified by the external world. Unpleasant thoughts seem to attract unpleasant events. Observe how often unfortunate things happen when you're in a foul mood. Truly, we create our own reality.

Thus, to recap and clarify, the process of self-hypnosis consists of two stages. *First* we induce in ourselves a state of hypnosis and *second* we utilize the state to focus on some purpose or goal. This simple distinction has not received sufficient emphasis in many prior books and articles.

For example, we can induce a state of hypnosis simply by quieting and slowing ourselves down. This requires the three ingredients of motivation, relaxation, and concentration. We stay alert, but not to the usual things. Our attention shifts to our inner voice, inner pictures, or inner sensations. Some people accomplish this naturally by closing their eyes and simply doing it. Others find it easier to employ a few of the many "induction methods." Remember that selecting an induction method, like choosing a mate, is a highly personal affair. Experiment with several methods, and gradually move to the one or two that feel the best.

The induction method is just a way of allowing oneself to get a little more quiet and relaxed than usual. Beginners may spend five minutes to half an hour doing the induction. As one becomes more skilled, induction time can be shortened to anywhere from a few seconds to a minute or two.

Once a mild hypnotic state is achieved, it can be deepened or not, depending on what one wishes to accomplish. Problem solving and memory recall are best performed in a mild hypnotic state, while certain forms of self-healing may require a deeper state. The deepening methods are just continuations of the induction methods, and can be similarly chosen and combined.

Next we come to the second stage of the technique: utilizing the hypnotic state to focus on some purpose or goal. Generally this is best accomplished by visualization: positive suggestions from the inner voice and optimistic pictures from the inner eye. It is most effective to work on just one item or goal per session, choosing it prior to inducing hypnosis. In later chapters we will explore in greater detail just which goals may be most relevant to your life. Any goal is permissible. There is one caution. Make sure what you are working towards is what you truly want. Self-hypnosis is very effective, and it works in subtle as well as direct ways. Be prepared for change!

There you have it: a description of self-hypnosis, a list of essential ingredients, and the basic two-stage technique. This, however, is only our introduction. The exact step-by-step method will be completely described in chapter 4. Before getting to that, we would first like to tell you a bit more about hypnosis in general, its common appearance in daily life, and how it got started on the world scene.

2

Hypnosis and Suggestion in Daily Life

Before we learn to make use of self-hypnosis we should become aware of the role hypnosis and suggestion are already playing in our lives. Self-hypnosis is not limited to the formal sessions where we sit down and say, "I'm going to hypnotize myself." Hypnosis and suggestion are not isolated phenomena. They are going on at some level almost continually throughout the day. This has a profound effect on how we perceive the world. It colors our lives, and in many ways helps determine the kind of events that "happen" to us.

Most of us have had the experience of driving along in a car for many miles on a straight and monotonous road. Suddenly we "come to" and realize that we had begun to drift off into a different space, even to the point of sometimes losing control of the vehicle. We were becoming hypnotized. The process of hypnosis frequently involves a continual, monotonous repetition of stimuli. Chanting, rhythmic drums, staring at something, or even hearing a long-winded after-dinner speaker can bring on the same effect. One part of the mind goes to sleep while the other narrows down and focuses on a small area. We are not asleep, but we are unconscious of a large section of our reality. That absorption is actually a mild hypnotic state.

Observe children in front of a TV set. They are oblivious to almost everything. We ourselves are absorbed when we watch TV or movies, when we read a book, and frequently while we drive or perform mechanical chores. Even more commonly, we are absorbed whenever we daydream. At such times our consciousness is filled with the events of the past or of some imaginary future, and is oblivious to what is taking place in front of us. If you observe yourself throughout the day you may be quite surprised by how much of the day is spent daydreaming, or deeply absorbed in something. We are almost continually in a state of mild hypnosis!

It is this very quality of partial sleep that allows the mind to be ripe for suggestion. When we are very alert and aware we may be open to new things, but we are not very suggestible. When parts of us are asleep they can be imprinted with all kinds of suggestions, without our seeing that this is happening. We are profoundly influenced by suggestion just because we are unconscious so much of our lives. And it is our almost constant state of absorption or hypnosis which allows this to take place.

What exactly is suggestion? It is a message from some internal or external source indicating what one should do or how things should be, what is right and what is wrong. It is a message which helps to condition us.

Our conditioning comes from our parents, teachers, and friends; from books, newspapers, and movies; from politicians, from religion, from deep threads in our society. All of these make liberal use of suggestion to mold us into the beings that we now are. The more unconscious, absorbed, and hypnotized we are as we move about in our daily lives, the more totally we mirror these suggestions.

In a typical TV auto commercial hundreds of hours of research and many thousands of dollars go into the nuances of suggestion. Just the right person with just the right clothes, expression, gestures, words, and intonation reaches into our minds at levels of which we're not even aware. The technique of repetition is liberally employed, to say the least. You may think you're buying a car, but you may actually end up purchasing a disguised sex object.

The same sort of research goes into the packaging of supermarket food. The very atmosphere in a supermarket is conducive to hypnosis—the endless rows of pretty packages, the soft, innocuous music. Without realizing it, you are enticed by a well-calculated color on a package, by a picture or a set of words. The label may carry the suggestion that the product is nutritious and healthful (a leading breakfast cereal with a very nutritious-sounding name is 50 percent sugar). When we "decide" to buy something our decision may have very little to do with our true wants or needs.

The written word is filled with powerful suggestions, particularly when we feel it is coming from some authority. Books, magazines, and newspapers are continually barraging us with implicit suggestions of how things are, how they should be, and what we should and shouldn't do. Even a simple word such as "God" or "enemy" can overflow with suggestion, inspiring people to commit almost any act. "The Free World" and "The Imperialist Countries" both stand for the same geographic location, but each suggests something different about the nature of its political philosophies. Suggestive words allow us to feel comfortable with the belief that our limited outlook represents the "Truth." They can also fill us with feelings that certain people should be killed, or that the group to which we belong is superior. Propaganda, which is suggestion, flourishes most where the people are most hypnotized. The more unconscious we are the more easily we can be manipulated by the suggestions of the written word and of the media.

Religions have traditionally employed the power of suggestion to control lives. Most people on earth have a morality and a value system that comes directly from the tenets of some religion. Playing on the fear of death, the religions back up their suggestions in a powerful way. The promise of reward (heaven, immortality, a higher rebirth) and the threat of punishment (damnation, a lower rebirth) lend a great force to the manipulative power of religious suggestion. Even those who feel intellectually free of such suggestion are often deeply held in its grasp, as they sometimes find out later in life.

Thus, almost all our ideas of what is appropriate behavior come from suggestion. Although much of this suggestion comes from religion, from mass movements, and from the media, there remains another vast area in which suggestion operates daily: the realm of individual human relationships.

We are constantly sending conscious and unconscious messages to each other about how we would like each other to behave. Conscious suggestion is quite simple: "Why don't you take a rest, you look tired," or "Maybe we shouldn't dress so informally this evening." In conscious suggestion little is hidden; everything is straightforward.

The majority of messages, however, are sent through unconscious suggestion. That is the means we use to manipulate and control each other. The husband will indicate to the wife that if she greets him in the evening looking sexy she'll get rewarded, and if she doesn't, she'll get punished. He may indicate this with a word, with his physical bearing, with a look, a gesture, a tone of voice, or with things done or not done. The reward may be affection or approval, and the punishment is usually disapproval. The wife may in turn suggest to the husband that if he pays attention to her wants she'll reward him; otherwise she'll turn him off. The subtle threat of disapproval between intimates can be suggested in an enormous variety of ways. The whole process usually goes on quite unconsciously. In a sense, the husband and wife are employing the techniques of hypnosis as they engage in the dance (or the battle) of the sexes.

Perhaps nobody employs suggestion as much as a parent. Every day she or he is communicating over and over to the children that they should do this and not do that.

Sometimes these suggestions are verbal, but the more important ones are deep and nonverbal. The parent has power over the child to withhold affection and to make the child feel bad unless the suggestion is followed. So the child tends to take in the suggestion and make it his or her own. The suggestion may often bury itself deeply and push the person from within, even dominating his entire life without his realizing it. For example, if the father suggests by his entire bearing, "You must always strive towards some goal," the father's dictum may act in his son like a posthypnotic suggestion, pushing him relentlessly. If later the son reacts against this, drops out, and drifts aimlessly for years out of rebellion, he is still under the domination of that suggestion. To be driven by the suggestions of others, and to be in reaction against these suggestions—both are equally binding. Acting from the suggestions of parents, or in reaction against their suggestions, pervades all human relationships and is responsible for much strife and misery, particularly in man-woman relationships.

Let's take a simple example of how suggestion may operate to make a person ill. A man with an ulcer visits a doctor. Superficial questioning indicates that his life is going quite well; he is even expecting a promotion soon, and his family is quite pleased about this. The doctor, suspecting stress behind the ulcer, hypnotizes the patient. He suggests to the patient that he focus on the present moment to get in touch with his actual feelings. The patient finds, to his own surprise, that he is very nervous about the promotion, actually afraid of it and resisting it. But the suggestion coming from society and from his family has been that promotion is highly desirable, something to feel glad about. This suggestion has implanted in the man the ambition for getting ahead as a value, as something that "should be." And the value has made it difficult for him to see his true feeling, a feeling which he "shouldn't" have. He is torn, but doesn't know why, and this tension expresses itself in his stomach, bringing illness. That is a very common situation. Whenever there is a conflict between our values and the way we actually feel, stress is the inevitable result. We begin to see the role unconscious suggestion plays in creating stress.

Much of our stress comes not only from the suggestions of others, but from unconscious suggestions which we give ourselves. Conscious self-suggestion, intelligently employed, can be of great value, as we will see in later chapters. But our unconscious suggestions to ourselves can play havoc with our lives. It is therefore quite important that we learn to become conscious of them.

For some reason, most unconscious suggestions we give ourselves have a negative element to them. We've all observed those people who decide in advance that they are going to have an unpleasant time at a future gathering. When the time comes, their self-programming succeeds, and they are miserable. Or we may imagine ourselves being clumsy and inadequate in a new and unfamiliar situation. This, too, tends to fulfill itself. Impotence in males is often preceded by doubts about their ability to perform. These doubts tighten them, their fear threatens to come true, and they become still tighter. Many men have essentially hypnotized themselves into inadequacy. An overweight woman on a strict diet imagines herself going out to a special occasion dinner with friends and succumbing to the rich and plentiful food. When the time comes, she finds herself overwhelmed by desire, and indulges. Many of our cravings arise in just this fashion: we suggest to ourselves in advance through imagination that we will want something, and sure enough it happens as readily as if we'd been hypnotized into wanting it. In point of fact, we *have* been hypnotized, by our own imagination.

When we examine those things that really bother us we may discover even more how deeply suggestion pervades every aspect of our lives. To take a very simple example, a businessman gets upset because the stock market takes a nasty tumble. He has imbued the event with great importance. In his mind is a game which goes like this: "If the market goes up, I win; down, I lose." Whenever he loses he gets upset. He therefore sets himself up for getting upset a great deal of the time. He may invent a multitude of win-lose games. Perhaps he decides that if his daughter gets good marks, he wins; otherwise, he loses. Or if his wife seems content, he wins; if not, he loses. Or if his weight goes down, he wins; otherwise, he loses. The number of such games is endless. In each game we set ourselves up for conflict, frustration, and tension whenever we seem to be losing.

It is remarkable how arbitrary the games usually are. We create our own games, we make up the rules of what wins and what loses, and we suggest to ourselves with great vigor and many reinforcements all day long that to lose would be bad. Therefore we are perpetually weighing everything that happens to us in terms of all our win-lose games. We are in a constant state of anxiety that we might lose, particularly in the games which we have suggested to ourselves are very important.

For many people the most important games are their major dependencies. We find someone or something that gives us a great deal of pleasure or seeming security in an unstable world, and we immediately set up a game in which it is extremely important not to lose. The rules are simple: as long as we seem to be in control of whomever or whatever it is that gives us comfort, we are winning; whenever we are threatened with the loss of control, we are losing. This is called dependency, and has an enormous amount of anxiety attached to it. What we invariably forget is that the anxiety is unnecessary. It couldn't exist without the structure of the win-lose game. And the game is something *we* invent, *we* are responsible for, something which has such force and power in our lives only because we are suggesting to ourselves all day with the persistence of a TV commercial how important it is. Were these suggestions to cease the game would collapse, and along with it, our anxiety.

Negative suggestions lose their hold over us when we become conscious of them. When we are unconscious of such suggestions, whether they come from deep tradition, from our family or friends, or from ourselves, we tend to blame situations when we feel negative. To become suddenly conscious of the whole process, however, is to see that the negativity is coming from within ourselves. It is we who have created it, either by giving or by accepting the suggestion that something is "bad."

To see how we do this to ourselves is in a sense to dehypnotize ourselves. We realize that we have the power to create and color our own world, and equally we have the power to change it, to make it a different color.

Thus, the first step is to dehypnotize ourselves, to free ourselves from the power of unconscious negative suggestion. The next step is to use this energy of hypnosis consciously for positive, health-giving results. The same force which now may be creating anxiety and stress can be harnessed to dissolve the tension and lead us into a different way of being. We will soon discover how this can happen.

3

How Hypnosis Got Started and Became Accepted

Hypnotic or suggestive therapy is the oldest of all healing techniques. Some form of hypnosis has been an intimate part of man's experience over the last three thousand years. Anthropologists tell us that all known primitive cultures had some form of hypnotic process as part of their religious and/or healing activities. Tribal shamans, witch doctors, and religious leaders in all cultures have utilized hypnotic techniques to heal the sick and to get in touch with the deeper powers of nature.

Anthropologists and archeologists have found evidence of hypnotic procedures being used in Egypt over three thousand years ago which were very similar to those used today. The ancient Greeks made use of hypnotic techniques in consulting the Oracles. They also had "Sleep Temples" where warriors and noblemen were induced into hypnotic trances by temple maidens. The use of hypnotic states is also found interwoven through the histories of Hindu, Persian, and Yogic cultures, particularly in connection with meditative practices. Often primitive cultures utilized self-induced trance states in religious rituals and rites of passage. In many American Indian tribes the young warrior, after much ceremonial preparation, would isolate himself from the rest of the tribe and induce himself into a hypnotic state. He would attempt to have a mystical vision or a dream communion with the gods, which would mark his passage into adulthood.

The Old and New Testaments of the Bible are full of stories of miraculous healing by prophets speaking "holy words" and laying on hands, both of which can be viewed as basically hypnotic techniques. In the Middle Ages healing through touch and prayer became the major role of priests and kings. Throughout Europe healers would treat their patients in the biblical fashion, using prayer and laying-on of hands.

The fourteenth century saw a spawning of healers and practitioners of various kinds, all utilizing hypnotic practices as the basis of their healing art. The Catholic belief that illness and disease were caused by evil spirits led to frequent attempts to treat disease with exorcism and conjuration, which are fundamentally hypnotic techniques of a forceful nature.

The belief began to spread late in the fifteenth century that man's destiny (and his ills) were the result of the magnetic influence of astral bodies. The universe was seen to be filled with magnetic forces. Hypnotic states were thought to come from magnetism; a skilled use of magnets could cure all things.

From this source Franz Mesmer developed his theory of "Animal Magnetism." This "new method" attracted a large following in the late eighteenth century. Medical historians view Mesmer's work as the dividing point between prescientific hypnosis and its scientific application. Mesmer is considered to be the first to give recognition to the importance of systematic suggestion. He was also the first to see important aspects of the relationship between the hypnotist (healer) and his patient.

Yet Mesmer was far from scientific in his approach. At the height of his popularity he was treating mostly women suffering from hysteria. A common affliction in

Mesmer's time, hysteria is the expression of psychological problems as bodily symptoms such as hysterical blindness or paralysis. Hysterical difficulties were beginning to be viewed as highly sexual in nature. Mesmer therefore built a large magnet and began to gather groups of women together for treatment. In his "treatments," Mesmer entered the room impressively garbed in alchemist's clothing. He induced his female patients into a group trance and suggested that they unclothe and make bodily contact with his magnet. Sometimes he would fill a large tub with iron filings. Patients, sometimes as many as thirty at a time, held on to iron rods attached to this large magnet so as to receive the "magnetic flow." The patients were also connected to each other with cords. Mesmer would circulate and touch each person with a glass wand. Many reacted violently, developing seizures, jerks, moans, and orgasmiclike gyrations.

Although Mesmer's induction was rather successful in treating hysteric women, their husbands viewed it as seduction and, needless to say, Mesmer found himself deep in controversy. However, his unorthodox and questionable style did often succeed in curing people. So a commission was appointed by the French Royal Academy (one of whose members was Benjamin Franklin) to establish Mesmer's credibility or expose him as a quack once and for all. They did the latter. Yet even with the commission's negative findings, "mesmerism," as it began to be called, soon spread all over the world. The word "mesmerized" survives in many languages to this day.

Then in 1814 a physician-priest from India named Abbe' Faria came to Paris and amazed Europe by inducing hypnosis in over five thousand persons. But his real contribution lay in denying magnetism as the source of the cures. Instead he attributed them to psychological causes, primarily the mutual beliefs and cooperation of the patient and the healer. Faria's basic theories of hypnosis still hold true.

In the mid 1800s in India, the Scottish surgeon James

Esdaile used mesmerism for thousands of operations. Hundreds of these were major surgeries, whose standard mortality rate would have been 50 percent. The patients' mortality rate when mesmerized was only 5 percent.

In the latter part of the nineteenth century James Braid reexamined Mesmer's work and renamed the phenomenon "hypnosis," after the Greek word for sleep. Braid, like Faria, saw the origins of hypnosis to lie in the psychological realm rather than in physical magnetism. Shortly thereafter a distinguished French neurologist named Jean Martin Charcot, working with hysteria a bit more scientifically than Mesmer, claimed to find a close relationship between the effects of hypnosis and the easing of symptoms of hysteria. He unfortunately made the mistake of theorizing that only hysterics could be hypnotized. But investigators at the Nancy School in France were able to take the next step and view suggestibility from a broader perspective, which enabled them to have considerable practical success with the treatment of hysteria.

One of these investigators at the Nancy School was Jacque Liebeault, a country doctor whom some historians consider to be the real founder of suggestive therapies. To avoid ridicule from the public and from his colleagues, he gave his patients the option of either being treated with traditional methods for traditional fees, or being hypnotized without cost. His earnest and selfless efforts attracted the attention and support of other well-known practitioners, who would probably have remained critical of hypnosis if not for Liebeault's activities. He treated over twelve thousand patients at Nancy and developed many applications that have become some of the foundations of modern psychotherapy. One of the most important theoretical results of the work at the Nancy School was the concept that suggestion and suggestibility was a normal element of common, everyday behavior. Almost any normal person could be hypnotized, and the phenomenon was natural and healthy.

Hypnosis emerged as a scientific technique with scientific respectability in the late 1880s. Hippolyte Bernheim, a famous physician, visited the Nancy School and then published a book called *De La Suggestion*. In it he saw "suggestion" as the basis of all hypnotic phenomena. Because of Bernheim's high reputation many scientists quickly began to give hypnosis a second and more respectful look. A sense of its validity was beginning to spread throughout the world.

One man whose attention was attracted to hypnosis was a young Austrian physiologist named Sigmund Freud. His first encounter with hypnosis took place at Charcot's Paris clinic, and Freud was impressed enough to begin using hypnosis in his practice. However, he later abandoned it for his own technique of free association. The reason in part was that Freud had an authoritarian style which denied the sense of cooperation between healer and patient. Hence he met with much resistance from his patients when he employed hypnosis. It was left for others to continue the exploration of how best to use this powerful tool in the new and rapidly expanding fields of psychology and psychotherapy. In fact, hypnosis fell once again into mild disrepute, because the master had rejected it.

The very technique which had helped to spawn psychoanalysis and other accepted treatments was again suspect. Fanning the flames of this suspicion was the proliferation of stage hypnotists, who were not concerned, well-trained practitioners. They were instead entertainers, using the technique for its utmost humor, drama, and shock value. In addition, the newly appearing art form of motion pictures hopelessly distorted the concept of hypnosis. For added visual drama the filmmakers inaccurately portrayed hypnotists as being able to control people by putting them into a trance against their will. In actuality, the formal technique works only in consenting and trusting situations.

Despite these obstacles the scientific community took more and more interest in hypnosis, being presented with mounting evidence of its real value. Perhaps the major figure in modern hypnosis is Milton Erickson. He developed his own method, which used no standard ritual for induction, but did center around the word "trance." More recently, however, medical doctors employing Erickson's ideas have dropped the term "trance" because of the associations it tends to provoke. Instead, they use the more neutral word "relaxed."

Hypnosis gained great acceptance during World Wars I and II, when it was found to be a very successful way to treat shell shock and other emotional traumas in soldiers. Perhaps that helped contribute to the decision in 1955 by the British Medical Association to endorse the practice of hypnosis in medical school education. The American Medical Association soon followed suit. In 1958 the august American Psychological Association went even further and established hypnosis as a medical specialty, with its own certifying board of examiners. Since that time more and more conventional doctors and dentists, as well as psychologists, have begun using hypnosis in their practices.

In addition to its clinical uses, the technique has found wide acceptance as an experimental tool in basic research on mind and brain function. For example, hypnosis has brought areas of what has been called the "unconscious" out into the open, allowing a new accessibility to previously hidden reaches of the mind. It has also been used to determine the various "levels" at which different kinds of thought activity seem to take place. More recently, it has paved the way for the expanding research on biofeedback, acupuncture, meditation, and higher consciousness.

Self-hypnosis may be seen as a special kind of hypnosis, in which the subject himself controls the process. Some researchers go so far as to assert that even with outside help we basically hypnotize ourselves. In this view, all hypnosis is actually self-hypnosis in some fundamental way. But the particular phenomenon called self-hypnosis does have a special story of its own.

All through recorded history people have been able to

enter into unusual mental states, using an enormous variety of external practices. These were usually of a mystical or religious nature. But the actual process of self-hypnosis was first described in scientific terms by the Berlin Institute's renowned brain physiologist Oskar Vogt during the late 1800s. He found that some of his hypnotic subjects were able to "*put themselves* into a state which appeared very similar to a hypnotic state." When these subjects practiced certain short mental exercises on a daily basis, their fatigue, tension, and headaches were all reduced. Vogt concluded that self-hypnosis had definite clinical value.

It was in the early 1900s that Emile Coué began to popularize conscious autosuggestion. The phrase which became his trademark was, "Day by day, in every way, I am getting better and better." This phrase has survived today in the training done by Silva Mind Control. In fact, much of the success of activities like Silva Mind Control, Mind Dynamics, Dianetics, est, and others stems directly from the technique of self-hypnosis, often given another name.

During the 1920s J. H. Schultz used Vogt's data to introduce a technique which he named "autogenic training." That technique drew on descriptions he got from hypnotic subjects about what it actually felt like to be hypnotized—for example, heaviness and warmth in the limbs. He found that a subject could attain a hypnoticlike state by saying a series of phrases to herself such as, "My arms feel heavy and warm." Experimental data indicate that various types of measurable body changes can occur during this process. Recent studies, for example, have measured changes in blood sugar level and white blood cell count. Other studies have shown beneficial differences in EEG brain wave tests between subjects who have been practicing over a short-term versus a long-term basis. This would seem to indicate that the regular practice of self-hypnosis over longer periods of time brings about certain beneficial changes in one's life. Very recent research on Transcendental Meditation has found similar results.

One advantage of self-hypnosis is that it gives the individual a concrete method of putting himself into the relaxed state, and then using the state to achieve a specific goal. This has several important implications which coincide happily with the recent emphasis on holistic health practices.

Self-hypnosis puts the individual in charge of his or her own physiological processes. There is the sense that one can be one's own doctor. By learning to control what were previously thought to be automatic (autonomic) functions such as heartbeat and circulation, individuals can develop a new sense of responsibility for their own health. The awareness that we create our own disease, and that we can cure it, is revolutionizing our consciousness about how we relate to our own well-being.

II

Technique

4

How to Do It

Now that you've prepared yourself with a bit of understanding of how hypnosis works, it's time to begin actually doing it. To enhance your success it will help to set the stage properly. The initial conditions are often important.

First of all, *when* should you do hypnosis? If you are using it for a particular purpose, do it whenever you feel it's needed. You may want to center yourself and gather together your forces right before an important interview or a heavy encounter. Or perhaps after an emotional confrontation you might feel the urge to get in touch with your feelings. Self-hypnosis can be a most effective tool right before a period of maximum effort. Olympic athletes do this all the time. In other words, there are obvious times when hypnosis is useful for healing, centering, energizing, relaxing—make use of it whenever the situation demands.

If you are employing self-hypnosis for the more general purpose of stress reduction and relaxation there are certain times of the day which are more suitable than others. Hypnosis works best at the same time meditation and exercise work best: when the stomach is empty. Right before breakfast is a fine time. The calming effect of the hypnotic state can set a relaxed, positive tone which may

last throughout the day. It may affect the way you respond to
the various challenges of your life. Before dinner is also
good. The tensions of work, home, or school can be
smoothed out to pave the way for a relaxed dinner and a
creative evening, rather than the all-too-frequent cocktail
hour, overeating, and the mental dullness which tends to
follow.

The least recommended times would be right after
eating. Hypnosis works best with an alert, relaxed mind.
After eating more blood is shunted to the digestive organs,
less to the brain, and there is frequently fatigue or fullness.
You want to make yourself as comfortable as possible when
you hypnotize yourself. Wait at least a few hours after
eating.

Right before sleep is generally not a good time, either.
Hypnosis is so very relaxing that if you are already tired and
in need of sleep, you're likely to end up drifting into sleep
rather than hypnosis. However, if you have insomnia, bedtime would be a fine time to make use of the relaxing
qualities of hypnosis.

The next factor in setting the stage is *where* you do it.
Choose a place where you feel safe and comfortable. Physical order helps to center you, disorder makes it more
difficult. External disturbance should be kept to a
minimum. It's best not to have TV or music within hearing.
If phone interruptions are a problem you might consider
taking the phone off the hook for a few minutes.

Any comfortable physical position will do, but we
recommend not lying down. There is a tendency to fall
asleep when lying down and a much greater alertness when
you sit up. Physical posture has a strong effect on the quality
of consciousness. Try lying down, observing the quality of
your mind, and then sitting up. Notice the change. You don't
have to sit up rigidly straight. For some people a meditative
posture is best, with an erect yet relaxed back. For others a
good compromise might be a reclining chair. In short, be
quite comfortable, but sit, don't lie down.

Avoid doing self-hypnosis while in a moving vehicle.

To refrain from driving goes without saying, but even as a passenger you might well find that hypnosis has a negative effect on the vestibular, or balancing system of the body. It's a bit like being down in the cabin of a boat that's rocking in the ocean. If you don't see the horizon, you're more likely to get seasick. The body may have trouble centering into a quiet space with the constant outside stimulus of motion.

One way of making it easier for yourself to get into the hypnotic state is to choose a favorite chair, cushion, or place in a comfortable room and do your hypnosis there each time. The fact that you've been in hypnosis there before allows you to make a connection between the physical place and the mental state. These physical cues can be helpful just in themselves in making a smoother, more rapid transition from the ordinary to the hypnotic state. Just sit in your favorite hypnotic spot and without doing anything you already feel a lessening of tension. Having the same place is particularly important when you first begin your practice.

How often should you hypnotize yourself? In addition to doing it whenever needed, you might keep in touch with the hypnotic state once a day. It is really helpful to your overall well-being to enjoy a period in the day when the brain takes leave of its usual cares for a few minutes. This relaxes, refreshes, and replenishes the brain, leaving the organism with a very positive feeling. Keeping in touch daily will also make it easier for you to enter the hypnotic state quickly and effortlessly.

If you are using hypnosis for a specific purpose which has little urgency behind it, once a day is also recommended. For example, if you wish to increase the power of your memory, it helps to do hypnosis daily (if you can remember).

For more serious purposes, for goals which involve your physical and mental health, twice a day is recommended. Thus, if you are employing self-hypnosis in a program of stress reduction, you might hypnotize yourself before breakfast and before dinner.

In dealing with more severe physical maladies, increase the recommended sessions to three times a day. For example, if you are working with healing a bad cut or a chronic condition, or if you want to make sure that medication you are taking is operating most efficiently, hypnotize yourself before each meal. In some cases you might even add a fourth time before sleeping, so the suggestions you give yourself operate while you are asleep.

Finally, for extreme, temporary situations, such as an acute hay fever attack, bad poison oak, or a flare-up of severe asthma, you can give yourself quickie sessions once an hour. (These would be in addition to any other medical remedies you may be employing. Don't let hypnosis substitute for appropriate medical attention when needed, but use it as an aid to help speed up the healing process.)

Now we come to the actual act of hypnotizing yourself. There are three stages in getting there (recall that "there" is a familiar and common place we've all been to before [see chapter 2]). The first stage is called *induction*, and its purpose is to achieve an initial relaxation. Relaxation is like money: when you have a small amount, it's easier to get more. But it takes a little energy to get that first bit. There are many simple and effective methods of induction. Following induction, a *deepening method* is used to increase the relaxation and narrow the focus of the conscious mind. This makes you more open to suggestion. This is followed by the *transition plateau*, a comfortable and familiar resting place where you touch down before either going back out of hypnosis or moving towards some specific goal. Or, you may go from there into sleep if you wish.

There are many different ways of achieving each of these three stages. At the beginning you might wish to experiment with a variety of methods. After a short while you'll probably get a feeling for which ones work best. Eventually it's better to stick with just one or two methods for each stage. Using the same method each time will help you to reach hypnosis more quickly and efficiently.

Here are some of the most proven and successful induction methods for you to try out:

EYE FIXATION. In this simple method you merely focus your eyes on an object. You can choose a spot on the wall, a burning candle, anything that suits your fancy. A small, discreet object is usually best, something that's easy to focus on. It can be nearby or across the room. Experiment with what distance feels best. Observe the object in all its details, noting the subtleties of shape, color, and lighting. Focus for several minutes, until you get completely tired of it or utterly bored with it. Some people will want to focus for a longer period; others, particularly those who are more experienced, may need just a few seconds. When you feel you've had enough, shut your eyes, take a few deep breaths, and notice how much more relaxed you feel than when you started. (Each of these induction methods should be finished with the closing of the eyes and deep breathing.)

CONVERGENCE. This is a variation of eye fixation in which the object is closer to your eyes than six inches. It might even be the tip of your nose. This creates a certain tension in the eye muscles, so it's even more relaxing when you finally stop. Otherwise, proceed as above.

UPWARD GAZE. Similar to convergence, upward gaze is even more powerful for those who will do it. The head is erect and the eyes are rolled up as high as they will go, so you are looking up at your eyebrows. There may be mild discomfort. This is just what you are looking for. When you gaze upwards the muscles of the eye begin to vibrate at several beats per second—similar to the frequency of alpha waves, which you may remember are associated with a calm yet alert state of mind, perfect for hypnosis. Pictures of famous religious people and saints often show them with their eyes in this position; presumably it is an ancient method for achieving a meditative state. (It may also be useful when a forgotten bit of information from the past is desired. Ask people a question that requires them to look back into their memory, and observe how often they turn their gaze upwards.)

MONOTONY. This is a well-known technique with many possibilities for variation. Any repeated pattern or regular rhythm, if focused on for a while, tends to narrow the consciousness and induce a hypnotic state. The pattern may be auditory, such as a clock, a metronome, or dripping water. You just listen to the sound, allow it to fill you, and allow everything else to recede into the background. A monotonous visual stimulus works in exactly the same way. Just stare at something like a pendulum until you feel yourself getting tired of the monotony. Then you close your eyes and enjoy being relaxed. The famous hypnotist James Easdale used this technique by passing his hands repeatedly in front of a person's eyes. To this day people associate such dramatic motions with hypnotism, not realizing it's just the monotony that hypnotizes people.

CHANTING. When the repeated pattern is verbal and the subject himself is doing it, you have a chant. Almost all religions have made use of the power of saying words over and over in a rhythmic fashion, usually in a monotonous pitch. This quiets the mind and relaxes the body. Some words seem particularly effective, due to the quality of the sound or the spiritual suggestions in the meaning. Chanting can be particularly effective in a group. Choose any word, syllable, or phrase in any language you like. Say it out loud slowly, over and over, until you feel sufficiently relaxed to close your eyes.

PRAYER. The type of prayer useful in helping to induce the hypnotic state is the short, repeated prayer, often associated with the rosary. The Eastern Orthodox Church employs such prayer, and monks will sometimes spend days, weeks, or even years saying over and over, "Lord Jesus Christ, have mercy on me." As in chanting, the words in prayer may have powerful suggestive value. If you are at ease and comfortable with it, prayer is a fine induction method.

MANTRA. When the verbal rhythm becomes internalized instead of spoken, the chant becomes a mantra. Many people say a single Sanskrit word or phrase quietly to themselves over and over, to enter a meditative state. In inducing hypnosis there is no need to use a particular language or a particular word. The word "one" will work just as well as "Om" (unless your beliefs lend strong suggestibility to certain words). To employ mantra as an induction technique, sit comfortably and find some word or syllable that you enjoy saying over and over to yourself, letting the mind focus naturally and as effortlessly as possible on the mantra. Do this until you feel ready to move on. Regular meditators can enter hypnosis by meditating for a few minutes and then going to a deepening method.

HAND LEVITATION. As you are sitting, rest your hand comfortably on your knee. Look at a particular spot on your hand. Then imagine that your hand is getting very light, lighter, and lighter. Perhaps you imagine that it's filled with helium, or being held up by balloons. You feel it getting so light that it begins to rise without your forcing it, seemingly of its own accord. Continuing to feel lighter, the hand rises until it touches your face near the eyes, at which point you let your eyes close. Then you let your hand go back down to the knee, and relax. For many people this can be a powerful induction method, increasing suggestibility while at the same time showing what suggestion can do.

MUSCLE WEAKNESS. This method is related to the previous one. Place your hands in your lap and clasp your fingers together. Imagine they are stuck, glued together; picture vividly how inseparable they have become. You pull on them lightly and notice that they do indeed appear to be stuck together. You imagine that no matter how hard you try to separate them, you won't be able to. You prove this by trying for a while longer. Then, when you've shown yourself the power of your own suggestion to keep the hands locked, you close your eyes, relax, and let your hands go loose.

HEAD ROLL. This method is often used in group hypnosis. It is useful for those who may have some difficulty
with other methods, because it involves a physical movement that aids in relaxation. Sitting up comfortably with the
head erect, relax, and let the eyes close. The mental image
comes to mind of the neck getting soft and limp. To enhance
that image you allow your head to roll around in a circle. As
you continue rolling your head around you can feel its
weight more and more. The neck muscles are getting more
loose, limp, and relaxed. Continue for a few minutes, and
finish with the head in its most comfortable position, ready
to go on to a deepening method.

These are but a few of the possible induction methods.
Remember that you can make up your own variations,
experiment, and ultimately settle on just one or two favorite
methods.

Some people can become profoundly relaxed just on the
induction method. For most people, however, the deepening methods are an important means of going further into
hypnosis and making the mind more suggestible. Since the
mind is already relaxed, it is quite easy to go deeper. There
is no need to dwell on how deep you are getting, on whether
it will "work," or on what is supposed to be happening.
Merely relax and let happen whatever is happening. The
most suitable attitude is that whatever state you achieve at
any given moment is liable to be perfectly satisfactory for
your purposes. There is no need to make an effort; making
an effort negates relaxation. Here, then, are a few well-used
methods for deepening your state:

THE BREATHING METHOD. After induction your eyes are
now closed and your body more relaxed. You begin to
breathe in deeply, noting how very relaxing it is to breathe
out. You let your mind focus on the breathing. After a few
breaths you begin to count breaths, continuing to enjoy the
relaxation of each exhalation. You tell yourself that each

breath is relaxing you more and more. Suggest to yourself that by the time you reach ten you'll be in a state of very profound relaxation, each number taking you deeper. You relax because of the suggestion, but also for physiological reasons. Deep breathing causes hyperventilation, which means there is less carbon dioxide in the blood. This affects the acid-base balance in the system, leading to a quality of mental lightness and to a settling down of emotions. Any time during the day you want to feel more centered you can take a few deep breaths and notice the change.

THE STAIRCASE METHOD. From the relaxed state after induction imagine yourself standing at the top of a stairway that leads downward to no particular place. The stairs are covered with a thick, white, shag carpet, and you are barefoot. You begin in your mind walking down the stairs slowly, one step at a time. With each step you take you can feel yourself getting more relaxed. Suspended above the bannister every few feet are little pyramid-shaped signs. Each sign has a number, from one to five. The numbers indicate the level of hypnosis you have reached. There are five numbers, and you know that when you reach number five you'll be in a very deep state. You feel yourself getting deeper and deeper as you pass each number. The deeper you get the better you feel, and the better you feel the deeper you go. When you reach number five you are in a profoundly relaxed state.

THE ELEVATOR METHOD. For those who prefer to ride rather than walk, this is a variation on the staircase method. You imagine yourself at the top of a tall building in an elevator which begins to descend slowly. It is a comfortable elevator, a pleasing space to be in. In fact, you can furnish it with whatever appeals to you. You feel yourself sinking, and you count the floors as they slowly drift by. You feel yourself getting more and more relaxed as the elevator gets closer to the ground floor. Perhaps there might be ten floors; you know that when you reach the bottom you'll be in a state of deep relaxation.

THE ESCALATOR METHOD. In this variation of the downward movement you are standing on an escalator which is taking you slowly and gently down to a very comfortable and relaxing place on the floor below. You know it's very peaceful and quiet down there, and you can feel that peacefulness begin to envelop you as you descend closer to the bottom. You can also make use of numbers along the wall to indicate your progress, from one to five, as in the staircase method.

THE CAR TRIP. This somewhat different kind of deepening method involves imagining yourself getting into your car, starting the engine, and beginning to drive. You leave the city or town in which you live and drive until the traffic thins out. You are in the country now, and you can choose whatever kind of rural setting would make you feel comfortable and relaxed. It might be a quiet beach, a deep forest, a sunny meadow, a mountain hut, a lovely garden, a real place, or totally made-up. As your car gets near your destination, you begin to feel a deep tranquillity, and a quiet comfort settles over you, as if the place were beckoning for you to come and relax there. You arrive feeling deeply peaceful, get out of the car, and enjoy being in your place.

LEAVING AND RETURNING. This method is effective when used together with one of the other deepening methods. After getting to the bottom of the stairs or escalator, or after reaching your destination by car, you open your eyes for just an instant, see the room you are actually in, then close your eyes and return to your place. You tell yourself first that you are so relaxed that it will be difficult to leave your place, it will take some effort to open your eyes. You notice that after an instant of being back in the room you are glad to close your eyes again and return to the space in which you feel so very relaxed. You might do this several times, each time giving yourself the suggestion that your state will be even deeper when you return to your relaxed space.

OPTIONAL METHOD OF USING CASSETTES. An entirely different way of bringing yourself into the hypnotic state is to employ a tape recorder, particularly a convenient cassette. You may use a tape from a hypnotist, but a more flexible and personal way is to make your own tape, once you understand the induction and deepening procedure. Go at your own speed. If it takes you a long time to get relaxed, take plenty of time on the tape. Give yourself the verbal suggestions you most enjoy hearing, the ones that have significance for you. Once you reach the deepest level, leave yourself some time on the tape to enjoy the transition plateau. Then you can either bring yourself out later in the tape after a period of silence, or merely suggest that you will come out by yourself whenever you are ready.

On the tape you can suggest that you will succeed at hypnotizing yourself on your own. This can be a useful temporary help for those who have initial difficulties. In general, it's better to learn ultimately to be free of the tape. You can't be as creative when you are stuck to what a cassette is saying.

From the end of the deepening method you go into the *Transition Plateau*. Here is a comfortable and deeply relaxed space (an imagined physical place and a very real psychological space) which gives you a frame of reference, a place you can touch base on before trying to do anything specific with your hypnotic state. Just being in the transition plateau for a while without doing anything can have a soothing, nourishing effect on your whole being. Being there and having it as a place in your memory makes it easier to return next time to the hypnotic state.

You can choose to rest at the plateau until you feel as

relaxed as you'd like to be, or as relaxed as you need to be. It varies from person to person, and you'll find your level of relaxation won't be the same each time you hypnotize yourself. Many factors are involved, including what is going on in your daily life. It's best not to have standards, but just to accept however relaxed the deepening process allows you to be.

Your transition plateau may be a room at the bottom of the stairway, elevator, or escalator. Make it a comfortable room, furnish it to your taste with fireplace, cushions, comfortable lounging chairs, sauna, thick carpet, hi-fi—whatever environment you feel truly relaxed with. A safe, neutral spot.

Another effective place is a warm, comfortable, moist, enclosing, womblike fog (not recommended if you have claustrophobia!). You can feel yourself floating in this totally comforting fog, breathing it in and letting it fill not only your lungs but your whole body, every cell. The fog has a healing, nurturing property. Just by going into it and letting it fill you, you feel deeply nurtured, soothed, and relaxed. It feels superb just to float peacefully in the fog.

Instead of a fog, you might create a warm, misty steam room where you can't see very much. Or a lush hot tub, indoors or out, complete with epsom salts. Or your transition plateau can be the place in the country. You can be quiet there, or go wandering around, exploring the area. You can listen to music, pour yourself a drink—in short, anything goes as long as it's truly comfortable for you.

The induction, deepening, and transition plateau together constitute the first step: achieving the hypnotic state. As we have mentioned, just to do this alone would be a great benefit to your life. Hypnosis without any specific goal has a healing, stress-reducing quality. The first few times you hypnotize yourself, go just this far, stay in your transition plateau as long as you like, and then come out (coming-out procedures follow). Soon, you will feel comfortable and confident with these procedures, and then you'll be ready for the next step, which is to use hypnosis for some purpose, and to employ posthypnotic suggestions for the attainment of your particular goals.

A posthypnotic suggestion can be given from a hypnotist to a subject, or from yourself to yourself while you are in hypnosis. It is a suggestion designed to change the way you act, feel, respond, or think after you have been in hypnosis. It may be a suggestion to stop engaging in certain habits. It may involve the way you respond to the world. It may have to do with your own healing process. It may focus on things you are doing unknowingly which amplify the stress in your life.

Posthypnotic suggestions *work*. They work so well that it is important to be sure you really want the suggested goal, because you are likely to attain it. Several later chapters are devoted to helping you choose appropriate goals and to showing you which kinds of suggestion are most suitable. Making posthypnotic suggestions is an art. Be sure to read on before beginning to work on yourself. Use only positive suggestions!

Coming out of the hypnotic state is even more simple and foolproof than going in. Nobody in medical history has ever gotten stuck in the hypnotic state. By coming out gently and at the proper speed you can insure that you will feel alert and refreshed when you open your eyes.

One of the most common ways of leaving hypnosis is the reversal of the deepening method, step-by-step. You start from the transition plateau. From there you go back to your car, elevator, staircase, or whatever you used to get in. You drive back to the city, go up the staircase counting backwards, or in general reverse the procedure. As you count backwards suggest to yourself that you are getting more and more alert. Suggest also that you will feel wonderful, refreshed, and quite awake when you come out, and picture yourself feeling this way. (This is one posthypnotic suggestion you can employ right from the start.) Give yourself this suggestion several times as you are moving back towards the awakened state. And don't be in a big hurry to open your eyes, particularly when you are first learning these techniques. Coming out faster than your natural rhythms would like can result in a less comfortable feeling. Experiment and find your own proper rate.

When you're a bit more experienced you can try simpler, more rapid methods. Some people simply count backwards from five from whatever state they are in. When they reach one, they open their eyes with the same suggestions of feeling alert, refreshed, and relaxed. Another way is to visualize yourself back in the original setting, and then simply open your eyes to it. Some people eliminate the counting altogether, and simply tell themselves they'll be alert and refreshed when they open their eyes. However you come out, remember to make the suggestions that you will feel alert, refreshed, and relaxed. They are more important than the particular reversal method you use. And finally, we recommend that beginners take their time right after coming out of hypnosis and not rush off immediately to the busy activities and demands of life. (Wait until you are fully alert before driving or crossing a street.) Take a few moments after you come out of hypnosis to savor the difference in the quality of your consciousness. This difference may remain with you for a period of time. You have begun to discover a new tool for living.

AN ACTUAL INDUCTION

Here is an actual induction and deepening sequence to help you in getting started. You can read it over to yourself a few times, become familiar with it, and feel more confident in your initial sessions. Or, if you prefer, you can read it into a tape recorder, relax, and play it back when you are ready to be hypnotized.

The induction is actually a combination of three of the methods we have described: the Upward Gaze, the Mantra (which is in this case the repeated phrase "loose, limp, and relaxed"), and the Head Roll. In addition, this process will use two deepening methods, the Breathing Method and the Staircase. The maneuver of combining several methods into one sequence is called "chaining," and can be quite powerful, especially for beginners. Here, then, is the actual induction sequence:

"I am sitting comfortably in a chair. My arms and legs are uncrossed. My eyes are open, my head is held erect. I'm going to be focusing entirely on an inner experience; for the next several minutes the outside world can do whatever it wants to do. I need only concern myself with my own inner experience.

"With my head erect and still, I gradually allow my eyes to move upwards, looking higher and higher upward until I can finally see my eyebrows. As I'm looking I begin to notice a slight strain in the muscles. I begin to look closer and closer at the eyebrows, to actually see individual hairs, to see the color of the eyebrows. I begin to notice that strain more and more; I feel the strain up near the bridge of my nose. I feel the strain up in the forehead. I feel the strain behind the eyes. I feel a slight vibration as the muscles are trying to reach their limit. As I'm looking at my eyebrows and straining, I notice that whenever I blink it feels very good. I keep looking at my eyebrows. It's somewhat uncomfortable, but whenever I blink it feels good. In fact, if I blink and hold my eyes shut for a moment or two it feels very good. And as I keep looking harder and harder at my eyebrows, the idea of just closing my eyes completely becomes more and more appealing. The idea of holding this tension becomes less interesting. The idea of continuing to gaze at my eyebrows as I'm doing now with great difficulty gives way to how nice it would be to let my eyes close completely. And feeling, as they close completely, how very relaxed I feel. How wonderfully relaxed and enjoyable it feels to have my eyes closed completely now. Just staring into blank eyelids and enjoying that darkness. Enjoying that comfort. Enjoying that release and feeling good. In fact, I feel more relaxed now that my eyes are closed. The muscles feel more loose and limp, and it feels good.

"In fact, the relaxation that I'm feeling now in my head is beginning to spread throughout my body. My whole body is beginning to feel more loose, and limp, and relaxed. And that feels wonderful. And if I allow my head to roll around on my neck—ever so slightly at first—but gradually more and more—just allow my head to roll around and around, then my neck can also become loose, and limp, and relaxed. I can picture it in my mind's eye. I can picture my neck becoming loose, and limp, and relaxed. I can see it begin-ning to sway. As my head continues to roll around in a circle I can feel the relaxation spreading. The looseness is getting more and more noticeable. The relaxation is becoming more noticeable. The neck is becoming loose, and limp, and relaxed. I can see it; I can feel it; and it feels wonderful. It feels heavenly.

"And this relaxation is beginning to spread through my whole body. My whole body is beginning to feel it. More and more loose, and limp, and relaxed. So I allow myself to enjoy this relaxation. And whenever I feel sufficiently relaxed I allow my head to come to a very comfortably situated spot on my shoulders—a very centered, comforta-ble spot. And I enjoy this relaxation, with my head now still. Now I'm ready to move on to an even deeper phase. I'm ready to allow relaxation to flow down from my neck to the area of my chest and my lungs, and to feel the air moving in and out with each breath. To feel the air filling my lungs as I inhale, and to feel how relaxing it is as the air leaves when I exhale. The air filling my lungs as I inhale, and getting me very relaxed as I exhale. Each exhalation getting me more and more deeply relaxed. And if I take a few still deeper breaths, if I take five very deep breaths, each one can get me more relaxed than before. With breath number one I feel very relaxed . . . and as the air goes out in breath number two, I feel even more relaxed . . . and as the air goes out in breath number three I feel extremely relaxed. And I know that when I reach five I'll be profoundly relaxed. With breath number four, the air goes out, and I feel wonderful, wonderfully relaxed. And now as breath number five comes I'm ready to feel profoundly relaxed. Now I can feel everything getting profoundly loose, extremely limp, superbly and wonderfully relaxed. And it feels wonderful. And now I find myself very loose, limp, and relaxed.

"And I find myself at the top of a long staircase that's leading downward, down to a very comfortable, enjoyable place. I'm at the top, barefoot, standing on a wonderful, rich, and luxurious shag carpet. And the carpet gets thicker as I look down the stairs. And I want to go down there. And I allow myself to begin walking slowly down, down, down, to greater and greater peace and relaxation. With each step I take I feel the comfort of the carpet on my feet. I feel my muscles getting more and more loose, limp, and relaxed. And as I descend I pass little numbered stations on the bannister of the staircase to remind me of my progress. I pass number one, a little number that lets me know where I am. And I'm feeling more relaxed . . . and I pass number two farther on down, and I'm feeling even more relaxed than before. I never realized there were so many different levels of relaxation. I never realized that I could achieve them so easily. But it's happening. I'm passing level number three and getting even more relaxed than before. And I know that when I pass level number five I'll be at the bottom of the staircase in a wonderful, relaxed, comfortable, and enjoyable place. And now I'm passing level four, and it feels marvelous. Now I'm reaching level five. It feels great, it feels wonderful, it feels profoundly loose, limp, relaxed, and I'm enjoying every minute of it. It's a wonderful spot to have reached, and I enjoy being here. And I'm going to take a few minutes to enjoy being in this wonderful, comfortable, relaxing place.

(Interval for experiencing the quiet)

"And after I've enjoyed myself in the quiet for a few moments, I begin to focus on whatever matter there is on hand. And if there is no particular work to do, I simply relax, and know that it's very healing, very healthy, very centering just to be in this relaxing space. If there is some work to do I can begin to focus on it now. I can focus on the one item that I've picked out ahead of time to put some energy into. I can begin dealing with it, with clarity and focus.

(Interval)

"And after I've done this for a few moments and gotten some resolution, some work done on the item for this session, I can begin to put that resolution, that resolve, into a suggestion for the future. I can tell myself how things are going to be, how I am going to be after the session is over. I know full well that this will happen, that what I suggest to myself will become true for me. So I make my resolution in the form of a posthypnotic suggestion, and feel good in knowing that this will occur. In fact, it's beginning to occur right now, and will continue to occur, even after the session is over. And that's what's beginning to happen now—the session is beginning to draw to a close.

"I feel good about what I've accomplished, about the relaxation I've achieved, the work I've done on the particular situation.

"And I gradually begin to ascend from this wonderful relaxing place. I begin climbing that stairway upward to greater and greater alertness. I pass level five, then four, then three, getting more and more alert as I do. Then two, then one, now I'm at the top of the staircase. And I feel more alert. I take a couple of breaths, and I realize that each breath is getting me more alert. I'm beginning to wake up a little; I feel my muscles, I can actually move my head and move my arms and legs a little, and feel my body beginning to become more attuned to being more alert. I can begin to stretch, feel myself becoming more and more alert. I can begin to roll my eyes around in my head and begin to realize that soon I'll begin putting them into focus. I realize that when I do open my eyes I'll feel wonderful, refreshed, and alert. Whenever I'm ready I can open my eyes slowly and feel wonderful, refreshed, and alert."

That concludes the sequence. This particular sequence can be modified in any way to suit your own individual needs. Whether it's put on tape or not, it might be a good idea to give yourself a posthypnotic suggestion that each time you do this it will get easier and easier; you will be able to do it more and more quickly. Eventually you will be able to do it very quickly. You can do whatever method or combination of methods that suits you, in whatever speed and style that suits you. This is an extremely individual kind of activity; ultimately no two people's induction sequences should be the same.

5

Helpful Hints
and Reassurance

There are several important things that you should know in doing self-hypnosis.

Perhaps the most important is that *all suggestions should be made in positive terms.* Let's say, for instance, that you're going to try to stop smoking. As a smoker, you have a kind of rhythm inside you that's saying, "Smoke, smoke, I need smoke, smoke. I need smoke over here." If you counter that with a negative rhythm, "Don't smoke, don't smoke, don't smoke!" you're just going to give force to that negative rhythm which you already have. If you're in pain and you say, "Don't hurt; my hand won't hurt," it's simply not going to work. In fact, your hand will probably hurt more.

The right way to do it is to replace these negative rhythms with positive rhythms. If you hit your hand and you don't want it to hurt, you redefine it: "Well, there is a warmth, there is a throbbing, there is a vibration. I can feel it tingling." If you have some kind of rash that is itching terribly, don't tell it not to itch. Instead, put your suggestion positively: "My skin is getting cool and becoming healed." The idea is to replace negative feelings by redefining them in positive terms. Pain, after all, is not just "pain," but a whole conglomerate of different sensations. It becomes "pain" when you interpret it as such. What happens is that we clump all these different sensations together and the mind goes, "Ah, pain!" In fact, the word "pain" should not be used at all in self-suggestion, because it is purely negative.

Likewise, telling yourself, "I will not be hungry, I will not be hungry!" will only result in reinforcing a destructive interpretation of messages from your nervous system. Useful suggestions would be along the lines of, "I am going to desire small portions of food, and eating these very delicious small portions is going to make my stomach warm and contented. These small portions are just what my stomach desires, and they will give me great satisfaction and contentment."

There are a number of other stumbling blocks to avoid. We've already talked about some of the simple ones, such as sitting in a comfortable position instead of lying down. That's because when you lie down, your body is getting mixed messages. It's not sure whether you're saying to go to sleep, or to meditate.

Another caution is to respect your natural body rhythms in doing self-hypnosis. Earlier, we explained that you should always use the same sequence of visualizations going out as you do going into hypnosis. But the speed of going in and out is worth emphasizing. If you go into self-hypnosis too fast, it's not going to work, because instead of tapping into a rhythm that is parasympathetic, that is comfortable and nurturing, the process becomes an irritant instead. That irritant can even be cumulative, so you can eventually teach yourself not to want to go into hypnosis! The effects of coming out too fast can be worse—ranging from a disturbance of your natural sleep pattern to headaches and nausea. You have to come out slowly and sit still for a few minutes. If you do experience headache or nausea after doing hypnosis, we can assure you that's the reason why— you came out too fast. The treatment for this is to go back in and come out more slowly. Just *how* slowly is difficult to say. As you become proficient, there is a cumulative lessening of the need to go through the specific sequence, but you cannot force this to happen quickly. You have to rely upon some of your natural wisdom.

There are other reasons why you may come out of hypnosis feeling uncomfortable. Sometimes the feeling will be a cramp, a temperature change, a feeling of oversensitivity of the skin in one area. That is very common. You most likely were in a bodily position that deprives a certain part of your body of oxygen. The symptoms are like "pins and needles." The answer is simply to move around a little bit.

There are times when you might come out of self-hypnosis with a feeling of depression, anger, or sadness. The feeling doesn't seem to be consistent with what's happening in your daily life at that moment. What's occurred is that you've tapped into an old emotional "connection" that you didn't process completely or handle satisfactorily in meditation. The way to deal with this is to go back into hypnosis for a moment and experience the feeling strongly. An image will come to you to help to regulate the feeling; watch it until it goes away. Here is an important learning process in which you use your self-hypnotic states to bring more and more things to consciousness that you have suppressed over the years. You don't have to go through a lot of age regression. Very often, it happens naturally.

Another problem that sometimes develops is the choice of an inappropriate induction or deepening technique. Throughout this book we're teaching many different techniques; they're not going to work for everyone. You need to work creatively to discover the best images for you. For some people, for instance, fog is a horrible image. Perhaps they had an accident in the fog; fog is the worst thing they could possibly imagine to get relaxed. To others, fog is beautiful and evokes all kinds of pleasant associations. Likewise, to some people, a stairway isn't going to be a good image because they once fell down the stairs. You have to

develop the images that are best for you. As we said, many of
the images will develop spontaneously as you practice
self-hypnosis.

Another problem is caused by unrealistic expectations.
You may simply be trying too hard. We've already talked
about that. The effort of trying keeps you at too high of a
functional consciousness level; the self-hypnotic process
doesn't work. The image you are working with might also be
inappropriate because it's too weak or too strong. While you
can't *demand* that something happen, you can't be too
subtle, either.

Now, some miscellaneous do's and don't's:

Practice self-hypnosis about twice a day. You'll find you
have a natural timing for it. Do it until it gets to be a strain
and then stop. Don't be a clock watcher; use your internal
clock. When it gets to be a struggle to keep the image, then
you're too tired and should stop.

Don't mix images; do one thing in one process. If you're
going into a process and you're going to do some self-
reinforcing, the self-nurturing kind of thing we call "ego
strengthening," don't decide in the middle that you're going
to give yourself suggestions to stop smoking. *One image in
one session.* Better yet, employ one image for a few days,
and then go on to the next task. Decide what you want to do
and stick with it for a while. Don't think, "I'm going to cure
all my problems with self-hypnosis, so Monday morning I'm
going to meditate on eating, and Monday night I'm going to
meditate on sleeping better, and Tuesday morning it'll be
smoking." That's not going to work.

Don't practice self-hypnosis just after you've eaten. It's
going to feel like you've swallowed a bowling ball. Self-
hypnosis slows down your digestive system.

Don't do it just before you go to bed; you may not be
able to sleep. Unless, of course, you're using it specifically
as an aid to sleep. Then what happens is that you go in, but
you don't come out—you just fall asleep. If you're not using
it to fall asleep, it's better not to do it in bed at night. The

best times are midmorning and midafternoon. Some people find it best just when they wake up in the morning. They get out of bed and then meditate. Others like to tie into universal energy in the environment and find that the best moments are the transition times in the environment: sunrise and sunset.

Everyone *always* comes out of hypnosis. You either come out or you fall asleep. If you feel stuck, if you open your eyes and feel like you cannot get oriented, or you just feel weak, it's probably because you missed a step, or you went in or came out too fast and your body hasn't caught up yet.

Very rarely, some people experience a little bit of a panic reaction, like, "If I do it any longer, something is going to happen to me." That is because there is an emotion they're tapping into, but don't want to face. Geneally speaking, try to get closer and closer to the feeling, and eventually you'll see the image of whatever it is, and it will go away. You may or may not remember the details of it after you come out, but you'll feel a lot more comfortable.

Remember, you're in control of the whole thing. You're in the driver's seat. No one is going to come up to you while you're meditating and whisper something in your ear so that every time the phone rings you're going to be a chicken!

As practitioners, we've sometimes gone through a process with people in which we gave them a suggestion they didn't want to do. Usually, we get nothing, or they'll simply come out of hypnosis. They were just not ready.

You can't make somebody do something he doesn't want to do. In stage hypnosis, when a person gets up on stage and is a chicken, he wants to do that. Yes, we mean he really wants—at some level—to run around and go "cluck, cluck!" And yes, the man who walks down from the stage and goes over and kisses that strange woman in the third row would really like to do that anyway. Consciously, there are no excuses, and no social permission, but hypnosis has given him the permission to do so, so he does it, and conveniently, he doesn't remember a thing. "Did I? No—of course not!" Stage hypnotists are skilled at finding natural hypnotic subjects with such desires.

In contrast, in self-hypnosis, you begin to integrate yourself, rather than losing integration. That's because you're tapping into more elements of your total personality, broadening your perspective on yourself and the world, and thereby becoming more in control of your life. You're *not* giving away control; you're actually mastering more control.

Many things happen in hypnosis. Images crop up, new emotional body connections occur. But you will only be fully conscious of and remember those things that you're ready to handle. You have some natural protection. You're not going to go in and have a "nightmare meditation" with horrible images and be haunted by them for days on end. All experiences under hypnosis will be positive. If something does happen, it will be most interesting and exciting but it will not be fearful, because you have natural floodgates. Your emotions are not going to come barreling right out at you and overwhelm you. Don't let yourself be bothered by a fear of that happening.

Now, some important medical do's and don't's. While self-hypnosis is very good for pain reduction, immediate pain reduction isn't always the wisest thing to do. Pain is the body's warning signal. It's giving us important data and to turn it off inappropriately can be dangerous. If you are in pain, and you want to use self-hypnosis for pain reduction rather than take pain killers, be sure that you know where the pain is coming from and what it is. If need be, consult with your doctor to be sure what's really happening. You wouldn't want to twist your back and through meditation stop the pain (which is very possible) and go on walking when you have something out of line and then *really hurt* yourself. If a cut hurts because it's getting infected, that pain is telling you something important; the same is true with headaches, stomachaches, and other conditions. *Always remember that self-hypnosis is an adjunct to your other medical and health practices.*

Finally, be discriminating with the use of the techniques you choose. Don't use a shotgun approach. Some of the techniques we describe are just not meant to be done all the time. A healing technique should be used only when you're really healing yourself. Some of the mind expansion and spiritual techniques, and the extra-ordinary states that can be induced through self-hypnosis, you wouldn't want to do every day because they will lose their specialness.

III

Everyday
Practical Uses

6

Stress Reduction, Relaxation, and Inner Peace

Katherine B. is a suburban housewife of thirty-seven with three children. The work of being a good mother, of running the household, of tending to her husband's emotional and physical needs, and of trying to be active in the community, is often more than she feels she can handle. She is beginning to develop a worn appearance, and is frequently quite irritable with her family. She never seems to have enough time to get everything done. She worries a lot about how to handle her life, about how to get out of the bind she's feeling, but that only leads to greater anxiety. This tension shows itself in the relationship with her husband. She seems not to be as interested in him as she once was. He in turn is more and more distracted by business, less and less interested in her. The realization of this brings about a new tightness in her, and she hears herself frequently responding to him in a complaining or harsh tone which she doesn't like in herself. In fact, she is becoming more and more impatient with the way she is and the way her life is going, which bears little resemblance to the glowing images she had of what married life would be like when she was courting. It seems to be a vicious circle: the more she doesn't like her life the more unattractive and turned-off she appears, and the more she affects her husband and others negatively. And then she likes her life even less. All her energy seems to be going into just keeping things together. She has nothing left over for herself, for her own wants and needs, for breaking out of this confining space.

When extra little traumas occur Katherine has no reserves to handle them. On this particular day she is supposed to do the grocery shopping. She is also supposed to pick up her children in several different places and bring them home, just in time to go to the airport to get her husband. He hates to be kept waiting. She is late with the groceries, and one of the children is not there on time to be picked up. Already delayed on her way to the airport, she keeps looking at her watch, feeling herself get tighter and tighter as the unusually heavy traffic slows her even more. Then she feels the car swerve and almost smash into another vehicle. She has a flat. Really upset now, she opens the trunk, only to find that her oldest son has borrowed the jack. She looks up in dismay at the heavily jammed traffic slowly moving by, thinks of her husband's wrath, and experiences a powerful wave of helplessness and dismay. The next day she is quite ill, a sickness which is accompanied by exhaustion that seems to last and last . . . .

Katherine is on her way to serious trouble unless something in her life changes dramatically.

Learning to handle stress is one of the most important lessons of being an adult. Many of us live in ways that are extremely stressful. We take on too many activities, and don't get enough real relaxation or sleep. We treat our bodies thoughtlessly, eating and drinking under stress. We don't get enough exercise. Our whole lifestyle contributes to a tense, nervous, tight way of being, which we try to mitigate with drugs and pills, only making the situation worse.

Self-hypnosis can serve as a powerful foundation for a totally new approach to this problem. But first it is important to get a feel for exactly what stress is and how it operates in us. On the psychological plane we are all acquainted with the feeling. It can display itself as a tightness, an anxiety, a fear of what the future may bring. It may be a trapped feeling, like being in a situation where there seems no reasonable way out. It often feels like there's too much to do and not enough time in which to do it. Under stress we sometimes feel very irritable, getting easily upset or angry. And as stress increases we may begin to feel that we simply can't cope any more.

Scientists have begun to investigate how stress operates in us physically. The nonphysical "feelings" we have been describing are intimately bound up in certain changes which take place in our bodies. These changes involve a whole series of predictable physical events. They include the secretion of certain chemicals into the bloodstream, a tightening of the muscles, and the rerouting of blood supplies so that muscles get more blood flow and the digestive system gets less. All of this is preparation so that our animal nature is more equipped to deal with what is felt as a threat.

Interestingly enough, it is not an outside event that causes stress in us. Rather, it is something our system does to itself, and it works like this: we're going along fairly smoothly, and then something happens. It might be a large or small crisis in our lives, a sudden or new pressure such as pressure from a job. This external pressure is called a trauma, and the body starts rallying its system to cope with it. If the trauma is physical, such as excessive cold, the skin density changes, the hair stands more erect, the blood vessels at the surfaces contract, and the breathing changes. These are called *coping mechanisms*, and their purpose is to bring the body back to a state of equilibrium. It doesn't matter whether the external trauma is physical or psychological; the coping mechanisms are always there to attempt to bring back balance. This is a very normal process which is going on all through the day.

Sometimes the coping mechanisms are not successful in

bringing balance. When they break down, a minor crisis occurs, and a second level of activity begins to operate: the *defense mechanisms*. Using the example of being cold, the body may now begin to shake, or we may start moving fast, curling up, or developing new energy to find shelter. Again, these defense mechanisms are a totally natural process designed to back up the coping mechanisms, to keep the delicate balance of our system from straying too far from normal.

So far we haven't yet reached the level of stress, which is quite far down the line in the series of events. When the coping and defense mechanisms are not able to bring balance and resolve the feeling of threat to the organism, a new event takes place: our sympathetic nervous system becomes hyper-aroused.

In ancient days, when the human animal lived a wild life with all its inherent dangers, there were frequent occasions when it was necessary to go instantly into action with a great deal of energy and efficiency. The action might be to fight or it might be to run, but in either case a sudden chemical stimulation increased the chances for survival. This fight-or-flight energy came from a particular part of the nervous system called the sympathetic nervous system. Something happened out there that was correctly inter-preted as a threat, arousing the sympathetic nervous system. Large quantities of electrochemical and hormonal energy were sent to the muscles, which enabled the animal to act quickly and instinctively. The energy was burned off, the threat was dealt with, and the system returned to normal.

Times have changed. As our minds and our lives have become more and more civilized and sophisticated, the physical threats have diminished greatly. Now we experi-ence much of what happens as another kind of threat—the threat to our ego, to our security, to our psychological being. But our sympathetic nervous system isn't interested in making fine distinctions; a threat is a threat. Therefore, any time we feel psychologically threatened, the same physical reactions take place that we have been describing. But now this energy has no useful place to go. So it turns inwards, and we eat ourselves up with it. When one gets the signal for action, the energy goes to the muscles, even when there's nothing that needs to be done. That energy gets bound up in the muscles, as a pocket of tightness, a contraction very much like a cramp. It seizes and doesn't let loose.

That is where stress lies. It does not come from any particular events. It is the inadequacy of our system for dealing with the feeling of an implied, rather than a physical, threat. This is actually fortunate for us, because we have very little control over events, but we do have access to our own internal mechanisms and the possibility of controlling them through self-hypnosis.

Our bodies have everything needed to bring us back to a balanced, unstressful state. The other part of our nervous system is called the parasympathetic nervous system, and it is designed to work in close harmony with and balance the sympathetic nervous system. The arousal of the parasympathetic is meant to happen naturally after the threat is over. Its response balances the sympathetic by relaxing the muscles and returning the chemistry to normal. The sympathetic is action-oriented; the parasympathetic is passive and healing. When the two are functioning healthily there is an alternation, a back and forth movement, that reflects in us the rhythmic cycles of the universe: day and night, summer and winter, life and death, intensity and relaxation. When this rhythm breaks down in our system, we have stress.

Because we are always on the go, because we seldom stop and allow things naturally to settle, because the machine is always finding new threats to its being, the parasympathetic nervous system seldom gets a chance to go into full operation. That means our machine hardly ever returns to its natural, balanced state. So two things are essential if we are to cope successfully with the problem of stress. First, there has to be a new way of channeling all the energy aroused by the sympathetic nervous system so we don't eat ourselves up inside. And second, we have to find a way of allowing the parasympathetic nervous system the space to function so that in operating it can establish the harmony now lacking.

Self-hypnosis can play a major role in cutting down on stress. It can serve as the cornerstone for a five-part program designed to bring a radical change to our system in a very powerful way. We should emphasize at the start that self-hypnosis by itself won't solve the problem of stress totally. *Every element in the five-part program is necessary* if you really want to have a balanced, healthy system.

However, the first and foremost element in the five-part stress reduction program is daily or twice-daily sessions of self-hypnosis. Just going into the hypnotic state, even without particular direction, and remaining there quietly, can have a profoundly relaxing effect on your system. Physiologically, the components of stress are reduced: the muscles relax, the adrenal secretion is slowed down, the stomach loses its tightness. In short, the parasympathetic nervous system finally has a chance to perform its healing function.

Daily life presents many challenges to our system; we provide further trauma with unceasing thoughts of how we'll handle things. Each time we worry it's like a small burst of stress, and the more we are actively engaged in coping and worrying how we'll cope, the more these bursts accumulate. So we keep fanning the flame of stress in our endless activity. Self-hypnosis, even undirected, is a respite, the one time in the day we stop fanning the flame. That rest is extremely important, and should not be confused with doing less total work. You can carry a truckload of bricks one at a time, enough to build a house, without too much strain. But try holding one brick in your outstretched hand for just a few moments and you'll see the rapidly wearing effect of uninterrupted strain on the muscles. They cry out for relief. The secret is short, frequent rests.

In the same way, our whole system cries out for an intermission, for respite, for time to heal itself. One might assume that sleep serves this function. But in far too many cases this fails to happen, because the unresolved problems of the daytime intrude at night. Our sleep is filled with the working out of these problems at a deeper level. Whenever we awaken less than refreshed, our sleep has not served its function of replenishing us. And to complicate matters, those who are most under stress and most need this replenishment tend to get the poorest-quality sleep.

We begin to see the importance of creating a time in the day which we give highest priority, a time for healing ourselves in the deepest, most general way—by doing nothing. The profound quality of quietness which can be achieved through undirected self-hypnosis is a most positive step towards reducing our stress. By being inactive for a short time daily we greatly enhance the efficiency and quality of our actions.

But there is still more that hyponosis can do for our stress if we choose to direct some of its energy into specific channels. On occasion we may become aware that certain muscles or muscle groups are particularly tense. Some people get tension headaches, in which the tightened muscles can be specifically located, perhaps just above or between the eyebrows. By pressing the muscles on the forehead, temples, scalp, and neck it is often easy to locate the center of tension. It then becomes an easy matter to direct your attention while under hypnosis to the particular muscles with the suggestion that they are already beginning to feel more relaxed and comfortable.

Another valuable technique, particularly useful if you feel agitated or nervous, is to decrease your adrenaline flow. Physiological and chemical changes occur, even at a cellular level, whenever we concentrate energy to a particular spot in the body. Hypnosis can greatly magnify this effect. If you care to actually picture the adrenal glands themselves, they are located just above the kidneys, on each side of your lower back. You can send them healing, calming energy, by envisioning the glands receiving nerve impulses which are relaxing them and slowing down their rate of secretion. But you don't have to be anatomical in your imagery. You might see yourself as a souped-up car which has been going very fast and is now beginning to slow down to a comfortable speed. Or you might imagine a thermometer in your system which indicates the adrenaline level, and picture it gradually going down.

On the psychological level you can direct the energies of hypnosis to decrease feelings of anxiety. While in the hypnotic state you are highly suggestible. Take advantage of this by telling yourself that things have had a habit of working out in the past, and they will work out appropriately this time, too. You can tell yourself that it's all right to feel whatever you happen to be feeling. Remind yourself that it isn't necessary to worry endlessly about your problems. You might give yourself a suggestion that whenever you begin what would normally be a long chain of worrying, you'll catch yourself, come to a full stop, and ask yourself if there is something that you would like to do about it *right now*. The suggestion continues that if so, you will take pleasure in doing what you can, but, if there is nothing right now to be done you will let go and relax. The important thing is to catch yourself early and frequently. You may be amazed to discover how freeing this can be.

Another valuable use for the focused energies of self-hypnosis is to help pinpoint the source of greatest stress. A person not in touch with a problematic area of his mind or body can waste an enormous amount of energy dealing with secondary matters. A single problem, such as an intimate relationship with unresolved conflicts, can spread its tightness into many other areas of living. A person who tries to resolve these other areas without dealing with the major relationship will probably find that nothing he or she does seems to get rid of that tight, unresolved, discontented feeling. Sometimes irritability over job security, relatives, health, or financial matters will spill over into relationships. If there is any doubt in your own mind as to where the major source of stress is, get into a deeply relaxed hypnotic state and suggest to yourself that the major anxiety source will come to you in a thought or in a dream.

We see how directed and undirected sessions of self-hypnosis will allow the parasympathetic function to operate in its healing, stress-reducing fashion. This will by itself have a most beneficial effect on the whole system. But a truly holistic approach to stress must involve other important areas of one's life, not the least of which is diet.

This second element in our five-part stress reduction program involves what we eat and the way we eat it. This is perhaps not the place for a lengthy discussion of nutrition. It is, nevertheless, important to see if you are inadvertently creating unnecessary stress with what you may take into your body. Drugs of any kind, whether they are for fighting illness, for fighting stress, or for getting high, put a great burden on the system, which reacts to them as a trauma. It is very difficult to become truly healthy while taking drugs. Drugs include caffeine, found in coffee, black tea, and cola drinks, which has a strong negative effect on the nervous system. Sugar also acts as a trauma to the body, stimulating an unneeded flow of adrenaline and all the chemical imbalance which follows in its wake. For some people, just to eliminate caffeine and sugar alone would bring about an impressive reduction in stress. Here, too, self-hypnosis can be of great benefit. If you want to change your eating habits, see chapter 7.

In general, the diet most suitable for combating stress is a natural diet. This would include plenty of whole grains, fresh vegetables, nuts, seeds, and fruits. Heavy proteins such as meat, fish, and dairy products should be eaten in moderation. Eat much fewer refined foods, packaged and processed foods, artificial flavors, preservatives, and colorings. Read up on nutrition and see what your body needs. In particular make sure to get plenty of the B complex vitamins (a very good source is nutritional yeast). A lack of these, as well as a lack of calcium or magnesium, can show itself as irritability or depression.

Other simple things to remember about food are to eat

slowly and chew your food well so that it gets properly digested. Don't put a strain on your system by eating a great deal at night. Eat small meals in general. And never eat when you feel emotional or upset. Stress shunts blood away from the digestive system, and stomachaches or undigested food may result. Be sensible and listen to your system. It knows quite well what you need—if you are able to hear its message.

The third element for reducing stress is a regular daily exercise of a slow, stretching kind. Yoga and Tai Chi would fit nicely into this category. Extending the muscles slowly to their limit helps release the little pockets of bound-up energy caused by the hyper-arousal of the sympathetic nervous system. Besides keeping the body healthy this lowers the stress level and helps bring about a calmer, more centered feeling.

The fourth element is a more vigorous exercise, often known as aerobic exercise. This may include running, jogging, swimming, bicycling, and some strenuous sports. To be effective this type of exercise should be done at least every other day. It should get the system moving so the heart is pumping blood at 120 to 130 beats per minute for at least twenty to thirty minutes. Besides keeping the cardiovascular system in prime shape, this exercise gives the fight-or-flight energy someplace to go. The release of energy helps lower the stress level. Also, by doing regular vigorous exercise, vitality is increased, and you are better able to deal with life problems, which are the real cause of your stress.

The fifth element in reducing stress is having some sense of philosophical or spiritual meaning to one's existence. It means to have a feeling of connectedness, of being in touch in some way with a process larger than that of one's day-to-day life. We'll speak more of this later on.

Once you begin to work on yourself in these five ways you'll discover that stress reduction is just the beginning. There are many stages of tightness. For example, as you are reading this, focus on an arm, a leg, or a muscle group in your face. Does it feel pretty much free of stress? Now put your attention there for a moment or two, and let it relax even more. If you try this you may see that there is a state of true relaxation which is deeper than mere freedom from stress. Real relaxation actually begins to release the stored-up tension from the sympathetic response. It is a movement into healing. On the physical plane, the body is loose and comfortable, the energy is flowing well and nourishing all its parts. Psychologically, the state of relaxation is not just a lack of anxiety or tension, but a comfortable, balanced, secure feeling, a sense of ease and well-being. It is a feeling of well-being that seems to have no particular cause. It is stress reduction carried a step further.

Self-hypnosis is the perfect tool to lead you into deeper levels of relaxation. It is a natural means, and it doesn't fall into the trap of pushing to relax. There was a book published once actually called *You Must Relax*. It is easy to see the fallacy here when put so blatantly. Yet many people in more subtle ways believe that relaxation involves some kind of effort. Effort and will are at bottom an attempt to change *this* to *that*. Such effort always involves at some level a pushing, a tightening, a movement in the opposite direction from relaxation. It doesn't matter what kind of an effort you are making, the end result is still the same: a denial of relaxation. Therefore, effort and will are not appropriate means of bringing about true relaxation. In self-hypnosis you accept the way you are at a given moment, without trying to change it. The change comes about by itself when you let go of all attempts to change. Another way of saying this is that when you give the sympathetic a rest, the parasympathetic will step in on its own.

"Knowing" that self-hypnosis helps bring about relaxation, however, won't do a thing by itself. You've got to sit down and do it. And if, like most people, you lead a busy life and don't schedule self-hypnosis regularly, you may find that you don't do it. To say, "I don't have enough time" is very misleading. You have time for that which has high priority. It is only in seeing how important it is to be relaxed that you give it priority. And when it has priority you will always find a few minutes each day to get into the self-hypnotic state, even when you are traveling or beset by many responsibilities. And it helps to remember that once you've learned to get into the state you don't need to go through the whole induction and deepening sequence. You can move almost immediately into the parasympathetic functioning without time-consuming techniques. This means you can allow the system to heal and relax itself in short periods of time, even five or ten minutes.

There are a number of techniques which can help you achieve greater levels of relaxation. These are all processes you can do while under self-hypnosis.

Visualizing relaxation actually brings it about. Besides merely floating in your fog, you can visualize floating in a quiet lagoon, or on a cloud, or in a warm, sensuous bath. As you float you can actually picture yourself getting more and more relaxed, and give yourself the suggestion that you'll be extremely relaxed when you return to your room. In your hypnotic state you can also visit a place where you once felt completely at ease, and recapture the same feeling. Or you can invent a totally imaginary place, filled with your favorite food, lounge chairs, cushions, furniture, or anything that makes you feel comfortable and at ease. You might even imagine that you are getting a deep, sensuous, relaxing massage, letting go of the last deep layers of tension stored up in your muscles.

Another process is to get into a supercomfortable position and go over each part of your body, working gradually up from the feet. With each part you come to—feet, calves, knees, thighs—focus your attention on it for a few moments and suggest that it is feeling loose, limp, warm, and heavy. Go all the way to the top of your scalp, making sure to allow plenty of time for everything along the way. This is actually a powerful induction and deepening technique, but we mention it here because of its great effectiveness in bringing deep levels of relaxation.

If you have ever been given an anesthetic with gas or a needle before an operation you can make use of the memory of that. In the hypnotic state suggest to yourself that you are breathing the gas or getting the shot, and that the same pleasant, drowsy feeling is rapidly coming over you and relaxing you totally. It is sometimes easier to recapture a former state than to invent a new one.

The deepening method of breathing is another especially useful tool for relaxation. In the hypnotic state take a number of deep breaths, slow, long, and regular, as deep as you can and still be comfortable. Tell yourself that each breath is bringing you to a new level of relaxation. Give yourself a posthypnotic suggestion that any time you feel in need of more relaxation all you have to do is stop what you are doing for just a moment, take three (or any number) deep breaths, and you will immediately experience the same relaxation that you are now experiencing. Even without hypnosis deep breathing works to relax the system, but hypnosis intensifies the effect.

We have been talking about a progression in changing our lives. We began with confronting the most obvious levels of tightness in our being, "reducing stress." The process continues with finding ways of achieving deeper levels of "relaxation." If we continue to take the process even further it may be possible to come upon that elusive quality which has been called "inner peace."

Occasionally we meet people with this rare quality. It is usually not something they were born with, but came about through living fully, with intelligence and compassion. They may occasionally become disturbed by surface events, but it feels like there is something solid, rich, and unshakable underneath it all. That feeling projects itself and is readily felt by others. It displays itself as concern for things which can be changed, and a ready acceptance when they cannot. Such people feel as if they have made their peace with the universe.

The movement towards inner peace is actually the evolution of the animal towards full maturity or adulthood.

A movement which begins with the reducing of stress and continues with the achieving of deeper relaxation now reaches its ultimate ripening in a transformed attitude towards living. Any person of any age can enter into this movement.

Something so profound as inner peace is not achieved simply by practicing a few techniques. Nevertheless, there are several procedures which you can do while under self-hypnosis which may give a flavor of what is to come. These procedures can perhaps put you in touch with a depth of inner quietness. They may allow you to feel a new sense of connection with the rest of the universe, which is in many ways what inner peace is all about.

THE HARMONY WITH THE EARTH PROCESS. When you reach the hypnotic state, picture yourself sitting in the middle of a field near a bubbling brook, surrounded by gracious trees and lovely flowers. You begin to reflect on the fact that you are part of this, and in total harmony with it. The warm sun shines down on all of it, including you, sending life-giving nourishment to everything without discrimination. The plants around you grow and some will nourish you; and perhaps when you die you will return to this same ground and nourish the earth. It is all one continuous, harmonious cycle, and you are an integral part of it.

THE ROSE PROCESS. This simple technique has a powerful effect on many people. While hypnotized you imagine a rose. You see in front of you a perfect, ideal flower, a thing of great beauty with a delicate fragrance. For a while you simply enjoy its utter perfection. Then you imagine the flower having a special magnetic quality. It begins to gather to itself all the negativity, all the problems and difficulties that have been intruding on your consciousness. You feel yourself becoming cleansed and purified as the rose continues to take into itself all your bad feelings. At this point you can imagine one of two things. Either the rose remains unsullied, absorbing and transforming the negativity into its own purity, or instead it finally explodes, and all the tribulations disappear in the explosion. Imagine whichever feels more comfortable to you.

THE ONENESS PROCESS. In the Harmony with the Earth Process you felt "part" of it all. The Oneness Process has you imagine going one step further: you *are* it all. You envision the fact that there is just one energy in the universe, an energy which takes many different forms. There is just this one encompassing intelligence, and you are an expression of it, along with everything else. Everything is natural, appropriate, and perfect, even in its seeming imperfection. Things are happening just the way they are supposed to. The way you are feeling at this very moment, you seem to be part of this perfection. You also remind yourself that some part of you at some level will continue to remember the truth of this—every moment of your life.

THE WATER LEVEL PROCESS. Imagine while hypnotized a series of scattered streams tumbling down a hillside. This might include a lofty waterfall and some churning, agitated cataracts. You follow the scattered, agitated energy of the water until it finally empties into a supremely quiet, tranquil pool or lake. The water has reached its level and now has no more need to rush and roar about. You remind yourself, while contemplating the tranquillity of the deep pool, that all of us sometimes go along like the water, passing through periods of seething, stormy discontent. And then you see those periods merging into the peacefulness of the undisturbed pool. You are moving towards rest, towards inner peace. Or, you can see the problems in your life as being ripples on the surface of the pool. Get in touch with just how deep the pool is, and what a large part of it is absolutely undisturbed by the surface agitation.

Try several of these processes and see which have the most significance for you. Employ your favorite or favorites regularly. You can suggest to yourself that the measure of serenity that you achieve in doing the process can begin to seep into your daily life, altering your attitudes, smoothing out your responses to difficult situations. If you work on yourself in this way a major transformation in your life will begin to occur.

7

Changing Harmful Habits

Many of you who read this book will have as your chief interest in hypnosis the possible means of ending some habit which you don't like. Since the mind is highly suggestible under hypnosis, can we merely suggest to ourselves that we'll stop smoking or eating too much, and have it actually work? The answer is that hypnosis *does* work remarkably well at helping to change harmful habits. However, it is not quite so simple as merely giving oneself the suggestion to stop doing something. Other factors are involved, and it would help first to examine briefly what habits are, and how they work.

Many of the general laws of the universe can be seen operating in ourselves. One such law is the tendency for patterns to repeat themselves, which, when it functions in our daily lives, we call habit. In the world of physics, actions continue to have reactions. Bodies in a particular state of motion tend to continue that way, unless acted upon. Matter continues to attract other matter. Things behave in repetitive, predictable ways.

In our daily lives we see that our existence is made up of a series of repeating patterns. These patterns help determine what we are, and keep our lives from degenerating into utter chaos. The way we interpret what we see and how we respond to it, the way we speak, the way we move, the way we communicate at every level, all involve learned behavior which repeats itself over and over, mostly at an unconscious level. This is habit. It gives a continuity to our lives, a predictability which helps us to keep order.

Habits can be broken down into some basic elements:

1. All habits are learned.

2. They tend to operate on an unconscious level.

3. They involve the repetition of similar behavior at regular intervals.

4. They perpetuate and reinforce themselves. The more you do something in a particular way the more the grooves are worn for you to continue doing it in the same way.

5. They are developed to fulfill needs. Whether or not they succeed in doing so is a separate issue. But the needs are there and the development of habits is one way of coping with them.

6. Once a habit has been established, any attempt to disrupt it meets with resistance. Anyone who has tried to change a long-standing habit has encountered this resistance in one form or another. Resistance to change is one of the powerful forces in the universe, balanced by the push towards newness and creativity. This resistance is felt as stress when we try to force ourselves to behave differently from usual. A part of the stress results from the fact that habits are developed to fulfill needs, and when the habit is broken the need remains unfulfilled.

7. Habits can be both positive and life-affirming or negative and life-denying. Correct visual interpretation and speech are habits which are essential to our well-being. Many of us, however, develop habits which destroy the health and sensitivity of the body, block our growth, create conflict, and make us lose touch with what it is we really need. Too many drugs or too much alcohol, unhealthy

eating habits, too many cigarettes—these are among the most prevalent negative habits in our culture.

What makes the existence of negative habits such an acute problem is that they tend to operate in a vicious circle, fueled by a need which is not being fulfilled. A person who eats excessively and compulsively may be hungry for nourishment at an emotional level. Not being aware of this true need, or not being able to deal with it directly, the person finds a temporary gratification and dulling of that empty feeling through the inadequate substitution of physical nourishment. Very soon the link becomes well established between feeling lonely, depressed, or anxious, and feeling a powerful urge to eat. By its nature the eating can never satisfy the emotional needs. All it accomplishes is to bring about a duller, more unhealthy body, which contributes an unpleasant quality to consciousness. This can stimulate even greater depression or loneliness. And the feeling of having desires which are out of control further increases the anxiety. To dull these feelings one eats yet more. Your weight soars, health declines, and the vicious circle is completed in what appears to be a bleak picture.

We can sense from all this that unless the need is somehow fulfilled in a way that doesn't create new problems, the vicious circle won't be broken. Many of the traditional ways of dealing with habits fail to take this important fact into account. This is why they don't work.

The use of "willpower" is probably the best example of an inadequate response to a situation we want to change. If you look closely at willpower you will see that it invariably involves resistance, fighting what is taking place. Imagine yourself with an itch that you are not supposed to scratch: "I mustn't scratch. I won't scratch, this is positively my last scratch . . . ." The end result is that the more you resist, the more powerful your desire becomes to scratch, and the more uncomfortable you become. Resisting something puts even more energy into it, nourishes it, perpetuates it, gives it life and continuity. You know what happens when you put a lot of energy into a boil, picking it and squeezing it. The boil enlarges—until you learn to withdraw your attention from it.

Therefore, the most important thing to bear in mind when dealing with a negative situation is: *don't fight it.* Since resistance takes many forms, it is well to become acquainted with the ways one fights negativity, so as to avoid the battle. Giving oneself negatively worded suggestions is a form of resistance, which adds even more charge to an already powerful habit. To say, for example, "I will not smoke, I must not smoke," feeds the habit, makes one more conscious of the desire, and increases the conflict. *The way suggestions are worded is of great importance*, and not only reflects our attitudes, but actually helps mold them.

If your attitude towards yourself is a negative one, or if you hate yourself for having an undesirable habit, or if it is not fundamentally OK with you that you are what you are, then this, too, feeds the habit. Feeling that you are not all right, that you have got to be different, automatically sets up a reaction which creates a stiffening and refusal to change. Paradoxically, the only way you will change is when you feel that it's all right to be the way you are. This can be easily misunderstood. Normally, one thinks in black and white terms: either I must fight and resist what I am in order to change, or I simply abandon all hope of becoming different and carry on in the same old way. If these were the only two alternatives we would be in serious trouble. Luckily, however, there is a third approach which does work.

To begin, it is essential to reduce the habit to its "lowest common denominator," to look at just what need the habit has been established to fulfill. Sit down in an undisturbed place when you have a bit of time for some serious self-examination. Don't just reflect, but actually use a pen and paper to give substance to your observations about yourself. Choose the habit that you want most to change. Carefully make a list of five reasons why you want to "break" the habit. Be as specific as possible. You might prefer at first to make a longer list of every reason you can think of, and then narrow it down to the five most important ones.

Susan, for example, was a twenty-eight-year-old woman who had been smoking since she was thirteen. She came to our clinic because her family doctor had advised her that her recurrent bronchitis was directly related to cigarettes. At that point, she realized that smoking had become a serious threat to her health.

The first task for Susan was to make a list of all the reasons why she wanted to stop smoking. Here is her first list:

1. I'll be healthier if I stop.
2. It's a dirty habit (ashes on clothes, etc.).
3. My breath smells bad.
4. It costs a substantial amount of money.
5. I have less stamina for exercise and play.
6. Foods don't taste as good.
7. A couple of friends have criticized me.
8. I don't like the feeling of being hooked on something.

Her second list was a consolidation of the key issues of the first list:

1. It's hurting my health and well-being.
2. It's hurting my feelings of independence and self-esteem.
3. It adversely affects my personal appearance.

Next, make a list of five reasons why you do not want to break the habit, why you choose to maintain that particular way of functioning. You may find as you do this that you tend to be in touch far more with the reasons for wanting to stop than with the reasons for wanting to continue. We say to ourselves, "I want to stop," as if this represents our only desire, and conveniently shove our reasons for wanting to continue into our unconscious mind, where they do a kind of hidden battle with our desire to stop. So this particular part of the exercise is very important, and requires a certain honesty with yourself and willingness to find out the truth. You must ask yourself, "What is the payoff, what am I getting out of behaving in this fashion?" What we find out can often go against the image we have of ourselves.

To see what we mean, let's continue with the example of Susan. She realized something surprising when she made the list of reasons for *not* wanting to stop smoking. She discovered that smoking was involved with several important basic needs. Here is her list:

1. It gives me oral gratification.
2. It's something to do with my hands.
3. It looks sophisticated.
4. It reduces my discomfort when I can't think of anything to say.
5. It makes me feel warm inside my throat.
6. It gives me a pleasant loose feeling.
7. I can see my breath.
8. It feels very secure to hold the pack.
9. It's fun to light the match.
10. It makes me feel that whatever I said was more profound if I said it while holding a cigarette.
11. I cannot cope with a stressful situation until I have a cigarette.
12. It makes me feel more like I belong.
13. I don't care enough about my body to stop.

Now, using the first two lists as a guide, make a third list of what needs the habit might be fulfilling. Then narrow it down to the one or two most important needs. If you have an image of what you should or shouldn't need this will get in the way of your observation. Try to "feel," without interference from the analyzing intellect, what your needs are. Write them down without censoring them.

Here are the most important needs as Susan saw them:

1. It relieves stress in social situations.
2. It adds to my self-confidence.
3. It's physically a good feeling.

Finally, think of all the ways you now have at your disposal that could fulfill these one or two important needs. Write them down, and take note of which ones seem the most appropriate, the most consistent with your growth and development.

In doing this, Susan came up with the following activities that she felt could fulfill these needs:

1. For relieving stress in social situations, I'll carry my small touchstone. That will give me something to do with my hands and also serve as a conversation piece.
2. For adding to my self-confidence, I'll change my hair to that cute new style and buy a few new outfits.
3. For physically feeling good, I'll chew sugarless gum or mints, as well as doing some deep breathing exercises every few hours.

Now take a step back and get an overview of the structure of habit. See clearly that you have needs, how the habit is adapted to try to fulfill these needs, and what you get out of it. Also see the pain it is causing you. Finally, observe that if you were able to substitute an alternative form of behavior which would fulfill these needs, then the habit would no longer be necessary.

Remind yourself also what we have discovered, that this substitution of one form of behavior for another will not be brought about by denial, suppression, or resistance. This leaves us with a simple and beautiful use for self-hypnosis which frees us from the inner struggle with habit.

The technique involves positive visualization. Put yourself into a hypnotic state. Now, using visualization, try to see as clearly as possible the way you would be if you were free from the habit you are interested in stopping.

Picture the way you would look, the way you would feel, and the way you would behave. If overeating is the problem, see yourself engaged in some activity, perhaps walking down the street, slim and attractive, with no thoughts of food. See yourself perhaps walking by a restaurant window with all your favorite foods on display, and then see yourself admiring the food for its beauty, and passing on undisturbed by desire. Feel the enjoyment of your slim, healthy body in just walking and moving. Feel how nice it is to be on good terms with your body, and to appreciate living in it.

If smoking is the problem, you might see yourself outdoors, walking briskly up the hill with plenty of endurance and a good, clean, expansive feeling in your lungs. The air is clean and smells delicious to your healthy lungs. You feel vital and alive, and totally free from the pull of the desire to smoke. Your energy is calm, you feel comfortable and at ease around other people. Use your imagination expansively to think of all the positive benefits which might emanate from changing your habit.

Notice that in our visualization there was no trace of denial. We are not fighting what we are. Instead, we are envisioning something positive. We are not putting ourselves down. We are gently suggesting alternatives. The hypnotic state will make the mind highly receptive to these alternative images. And whatever the habit, with a bit of care, you can come up with suitable images of yourself in a healthy state.

Next we become more specific, although even if we had stopped here much good would have been done. Recall the list of alternate ways of fulfilling your basic need(s), and in particular the most suitable way(s). Now begin to visualize yourself as clearly as you can, engaged in this self-nurturing activity. Picture yourself not only doing it, but feeling really good from doing it. When you have reinforced these positive images sufficiently, come out of the hypnotic state.

Then you can really help the process along in a powerful way. As soon as possible go out and do the last thing you visualized, the alternative method of fulfilling your need. This is such a helpful tool because of an interesting quality in the way suggestion works. If something is suggested and soon afterwards it happens, the power of suggestion is increased. Each success reinforces this useful power. So it really helps if there is reinforcement and support right near the beginning, to get started along a salutary route. Doing soon afterwards what was recently visualized accomplishes just this.

So far, so good. We have set the stage for a real change to come into our lives; we have created conditions which make it much more possible. Now it remains to be vigilant in avoiding the trap of fighting the habit head-on. Don't try to stop doing the negative habit in any way. All the good accomplished thus far would be sacrificed if denial and resistance entered at this point. Be very clear, in short, that it is truly all right for you to feel any desire and act on it. Let go of all feelings of self-recrimination and guilt. See if you can't sense that a different process is at work, one in which you have no need to stand over yourself with a cruel whip. That part of you, which stands guard over the rest to judge and punish, can simply evaporate. See how absolutely ineffective the old methods of resistance have been, and allow yourself fully to participate in this far gentler approach. If you really have an urge for that cigarette, smoke it and enjoy it!

If you are like most people, you will soon find out that your intense desire is beginning to wither away. Very shortly you find that, while you sometimes partake of the habit, you sometimes choose not to, without any pressure or conflict. If you are smoking, for example, you find that you are smoking perhaps half as much as before, without trying to stop. As time goes on you find that a new, positive rhythm is beginning to replace the negative rhythm in a natural, organic-feeling process which lacks the friction of inner conflict.

The reason this works is quite simple. Your need is

being fulfilled in a way that it never was in the battleground of the habit process. You are now consciously being kind to yourself, nurturing yourself by choosing consciously an activity which nourishes you. There are no contradictory feelings attached; you really want to be kind to yourself. Such an attitude is bound to succeed. This, combined with not fighting yourself any more, is the soil from which can grow new, more healthy patterns of behavior.

This is the essence of a healthy attitude. It also helps to have a few refinements at your fingertips to help the process speedily along. We'll use for convenience the example of a smoker, although any habit may be substituted.

Think first of what it is you are really craving, what need smoking is attempting (unsuccessfully) to fulfill. Perhaps, for example, you may feel the cigarette at your lips to be, among other things, nurturing. You may also feel a warm, relaxed feeling inside with each puff. Finally, when you exhale, the smoke may prove to you as you observe its emergence from the nose and mouth, that you are alive. (It is very curious to note that almost no blind people smoke.)

It may now interest you to find alternative nurturing, relaxing, and life-confirming activities which you might do if there were no urge to smoke. Begin to play around a little and say to yourself, "All right, you can smoke whenever you please, but you also have to go through a little ritual before each cigarette. You're doing this voluntarily, because you want to, you are really interested in exploring new approaches."

Now invent a couple of rituals. You might, for instance, decide that with every craving for a cigarette, you will step outside as soon as possible and take ten slow, deep breaths, focusing on the air as it enters and leaves your lungs. You might have as an alternative ritual taking a ball or some unobtrusive toy in your hand and playing with it for one minute very consciously, giving it your full attention. After the ritual you get to choose whether or not to smoke, and either alternative is OK.

Begin to discover an interesting form of substitution. Normally, *experience* something different, change the *activity*; that is, substitute one activity for another. In this case you change the way you feel by changing the perspective regarding that activity. Let's say you have an itch. Normally you might regard it as an "itch" which has to be "scratched." Instead, try redefining it as a delicious tingling sensation on your arm, a sensuous delight to be savored and appreciated. And since it has a certain tension connected with it, relieve that tension by blowing on it instead of scratching it.

Often the very names we use for things make us resist them because they carry the charge of a negative connotation in our minds. Redefining a sensation in different terms can often help create a fresh and enlightening perspective. Redefining "appetite for food," normally something which automatically demands satisfaction, as "an intensity of feeling, stimulated by thought, which we can observe for its own sake," allows us to live with the feeling without the need to *do* something about it.

Along with changing attitudes, we can utilize self-hypnosis to change rhythms. If you explore the dynamics of the habit process, you come across a "regular" pattern of activity. Most habits have a regular structure to them. We eat every three hours regardless of our body's messages; or our inner clock lets us know within a half hour of each cigarette that it's time for the next one. Once you become acquainted with the negative rhythm patterns it is easy to make use of the self-hypnotic state to suggest positive rhythm patterns that succeed in balancing out the negative ones, while creating little or no disturbance in your life. For example, you might suggest that every three hours you take a break and have a small amount of some healthy snack that doesn't breed compulsive eating for you, such as yogurt.

Another specific avenue of approach is to use the hypnotic state to restructure your activities, making a real commitment to a beneficial lifestyle. You may, for example, sense that getting up earlier in the morning is more compatible with what it is you envision as your new, positive lifestyle. It would then be easy to visualize the joys of getting up early, watching it get light in the quiet before the day's bustle starts. Or perhaps you see yourself getting some useful work done in the fresh, early morning hours. Use positive visualization to make specific changes in the habitual patterns of behavior which may be the components of your larger habit. These separate activities are part of a single movement, which is a commitment to a lifestyle which is beneficial to your total being.

Allow yourself while in the hypnotic state to experience some affirmations, some reminders of positive ways of being. Spend a few minutes each day in the hypnotic state visualizing for yourself what a positive, nurturing lifestyle would be like. With such reinforcement it is harder to light up so many cigarettes.

There are several specific processes which may be used in dealing with bad habits. For instance:

THE POISONOUS SUBSTANCE PROCESS may prove an added strength if your habit is one which makes you feel like you are taking poisons into your body and you would like to stop. While in the self-hypnotic state, come in close contact with the facts which you may have been subtly avoiding—that the substance is a real poison to your system. In the case of smoking, for example, visualize the coarse, impure smoke filling up your lungs and settling into a growing layer of black sludge, clogging up your pores and destroying the smooth flow of your system. Really see it vividly. Then imagine the many toxins from your lungs entering the bloodstream, spreading out over the entire body and flooding all the vital organs with life-denying poisons. You can even get down to the cellular level, feeling the oxygen deprivation of the individual cells, that suffocating feeling found in the immediacy of a toxic atmosphere.

All this sounds like a dire contradiction of our plea for positive suggestions. The process continues, however, with a vigorous new visualization of the way you would rather be, free from all poisons. You imagine yourself breathing in the fresh, nourishing air, which fills the remotest pores of your healthy, expansive lungs. You observe the nourishing oxygen from the air spreading into the blood stream, a life force which gives vital sustenance to every cell. You feel the very smallest units in your body, the cells, singing their song of life, well-fed and flourishing.

The juxtaposition of these two images—the frightening poison and the comforting health—is an extremely effective tool in laying before yourself the blatant facts. Certain lifestyles are death oriented, while others are life oriented. Seeing the two in stark relief against each other can strike home at a level deeper than the intellect chooses to venture.

COMMUNION WITH FOOD PROCESS. If your habit involves eating, you can utilize self-hypnosis to create a healthy new attitude towards your food, one which in itself will alter your eating patterns. Our normal method of ingestion is to shovel food into our mouths more or less unaware of what it tastes like. This pretty much guarantees that it will fail to nurture us. In the Communion with Food Process you begin to teach yourself new patterns of relating to food. Get a good, ripe piece of fruit of a kind that you really enjoy. Place it in front of you, and then go into the hypnotic state. From there, picture the fruit as an expression of life, with a life essence just like your own. It has an individual integrity; there is no other piece of fruit anywhere quite like it. Like other living things it takes nourishment, it eliminates, it is part of an ongoing reproductive process, it is conscious. While still in the state, take hold of the fruit, caress it, and slowly take a bite of it, feeling it almost melt in your mouth. It's like making love to your food. You feel the life essence of the fruit beginning to merge with your own essence in one of the most intimate processes we know. Your mind is not thinking about other things, nor is it comparing the flavor of the fruit with anything else. You suggest to yourself that this quality of savoring and merging can be present whenever you eat.

To eat in this way is to get truly nurtured from your food. Many people who overeat would find that if they allow themselves to eat whatever they want and make an agreement with themselves to eat slowly in this fashion, they would get their needs more fulfilled while eating less.

With these tools at our disposal, let us look at an actual case history. John R. is a thirty-seven-year-old business executive who recalled smoking since he was in his early teens. During most of his adult life he has averaged between one and two packs per day, even more on particularly trying days on the job. The cumulative years of smoking had clearly become a danger to his health. After attending one of our self-hypnosis courses John decided to begin a habit-reduction program. He began his personal program by doing the pen and paper exercise, which revealed that his major need was a "self-feeding" or nurturing one. Under stress he felt the need to be "comforted and warmed all inside." He recalled his mother giving him warm milk and hot soup as a child whenever he was ill. The smoking quickly replaced his mother's attention when he grew into adolescence.

As an adult, he continued to rely on smoking, as the pressures of living made his needs feel stronger. Clear about the nature of these needs, he began his self-hypnosis by getting relaxed and imagining himself being nurtured and protected by a loving maternal figure. He focused on the feeling of being "all warm inside." At the same time he visualized himself feeling alive and energized, felt himself breathing the clean, refreshing air, and pictured all this going on without the slightest craving for nicotine. Every time he felt the urge for a cigarette he did this process. Then if he still felt the need to smoke, he would go ahead and do so. After one week, he reported smoking about half as many cigarettes. About one out of two times he was fulfilling his need "naturally" without a cigarette. After four weeks, he was free from smoking, the pressures of his life were more in perspective, he felt "less stressful" and looked more relaxed.

John has an excellent chance of remaining with his healthier lifestyle. His cravings were actually altered in the processes of fulfilling his needs. He reported that in the past when he imagined a cigarette, the feeling was automatically accompanied by a desire for the immediacy of sensation. This has now altered. He still sometimes thinks of a cigarette—only now he pictures not only the way it would feel at the moment, but also what it would do to his system. He also imagines the mechanisms of guilt, anxiety, and conflict being set into motion with the cigarette, and finds that when he contemplates the total effect of the cigarette, it isn't very appealing to him. He isn't feeling deprived of anything; in order to feel deprived you have to want something, and his desire has withered away.

John also mentioned his enjoyment in watching his friends light up. In the past he had always felt somewhat envious every time he encountered a healthy nonsmoker with a good body. He would compare the person to himself and feel the tightness of inadequacy. Now the tables are turned. Without feeling righteous or superior, John sees his friends indulge and feels reminded each time that he is now being kind to his body. He feels grateful each time he is reminded, so that he actually welcomes the occasion to be around those who still smoke.

It has now been almost a year since John began his program. For him it feels like the struggle is a thing of the past. Free of the craving for tobacco, he is very comfortable with his new lifestyle. Other changes, somewhat unexpected, have occurred in his life. In the process of moving out of the enclosed world of "I crave tobacco but I mustn't have it," John discovered that there are other, more effective ways of relating to problems than by struggling, fighting, and resisting. He has discovered how resistance perpetuates the problem, while the softer approach he used to free himself from the habit has many implications in his daily life. His relationships with his wife and children have improved positively, first because he feels healthier and more alive, and second because stopping smoking has shown him that the only way to be really free of a problem is to allow the situation to unfold without fighting it. Your own habits can be perceived not as something to be gotten rid of, but rather as a fine opportunity for learning and growth.

8

Self-Hypnosis for Self-Healing

Have you ever cut yourself and then observed daily the marvelous process of healing? "Health," "healing," "hale," "holy," "whole," "holistic": these related words come from the same original Greek root. They stand for something so natural that it happens by itself—whenever we don't interfere. So, it's not that we are consciously *doing something*; the cut heals by itself miraculously if we *stop interfering* with the process. In a sense the essence of what is called "self-healing" is actually learning what it means to stop interfering, whether the problem is a cut, physical illness, or psychological disease.

"Interfering" may take many forms. It may be simply not keeping an infection clean. It may be a continual bombardment of the digestive system with too much food or the wrong foods. It may be the taking of drugs, for medical reasons or otherwise. And in many cases it consists of the psychological equivalent of taking in and digesting harmful substances. The only difference is that now the intake is not physically tangible.

This latter kind of harmful intake, which prevents our wounds or our diseases from healing, takes the form of pessimistic thoughts, negative images, and unhealthy pictures. We will show you in this chapter how very important is the quality of our images in either inhibiting or promoting the natural healing process.

How, specifically, do we use a visual meditation like self-hypnosis to allow and encourage healing? The rules and methods are easy; it merely takes practice, like learning to cook. With practice you can get better and better.

First, it is important to get in touch with the source of the problem. The negative situations in our lives are seldom caused by a single factor; there are many forces that combine to create a situation. Having a bad day, having a cold, having a bicycle accident, or having a cancerous tumor—all of these can be seen as resulting from the totality of our response to life. We are often participating in a negative situation, keeping it going without realizing it. A person getting treatment for cancer will often, while the treatment is going on, be continuing the very process that started the cancer in the first place.

For example, someone might be fed up with the behavior of his or her mate without knowing how to deal with the negative feelings. These feelings turn inward and begin to accumulate as toxicity in the system, and no external treatment will work well without dealing also with this toxic accumulation. So a clear overview is necessary to avoid the superficiality of responding merely to symptoms.

Second, it is necessary to think positively and see the situation improving. The visual image is so powerful that it can literally bring into being physically whatever we're seeing mentally. So if you're thinking illness, thinking about cancer spreading all over you, that can become the fact. On the other hand, if you encourage only positive thoughts and suggestions, the reverse begins to be true. This doesn't mean to fight, suppress, or resist negative thoughts. They are there and part of life. To resist them just helps to perpetuate them, as well as to create still more internal friction—the major problem to begin with. Instead, become conscious of negative images (for when they are unconscious the real harm is done). Be aware of them and let them go without feeding them. That way they'll lose their potency. Then you can begin to play with more positive imagery, nourish it, and let it fill you. Thus, the secret is to be aware of the negative, but favor and choose to focus on the positive.

So, first is clear observation, second is having only positive suggestions, and third is thinking in a distinctly visual way. This means actually imagining the scene pictorially in as specifically detailed a fashion as possible. If you have medical training you see a tumor as a clump of cells. With other training you might see it differently. The image might be a devil with a forked stick, a crab eating away at you—however simple or silly, that is the image to work with. In fact, a seemingly ridiculous image can often be quite effective.

The important thing is to have a really vivid picture, and to imagine the situation getting better. So if it's a picture of crabs attacking you, you can imagine a fisherman coming around with a net and scooping them up. Or you can imagine the crabs just shriveling up and disappearing. Whatever is real and vivid for you is what you should do. That is why the technique involves a total responsibility on your part. No person or book will give you the suggestion that is optimal for you. The most appropriate, significant, and powerful images bubble up naturally from deep within your internal being. Allow your image to emerge, and be creative with how it is to get better. The more vigorous and powerful you make your images of healing, the more healing you will experience.

A doctor would tend to get images of an actual anatomical situation, because he's seen tissues and blood cells. Some doctors recommend that people with cancer imagine their body's own medical defenses in the form of white blood cells, which are called lymphocytes, attacking the cancer cells and destroying them. One medical theory states that a few normal cells become cancerous every so often in our body as a matter of course, and that the healthy body has a surveillance and defense system which takes care of them without problem. That's what is happening medically when a remission occurs. If you are on chemotherapy you can imagine the drug as cavalry coming in with swords and guns, attacking all the cancer cells. If the medical model is real for you, we urge you to use it. But whatever form the image takes, put some energy into it and continually see the situation getting better in your visualization.

In addition to helping with serious illnesses, self-hypnosis is useful for minor problems. Here is an example of what self-healing might mean in everyday activity. Imagine a person out in the garden digging. This is someone who's in a hurry, who has a lot of work to do. He begins working faster and faster, until he agitatedly stubs his toe. But he keeps on going, and then a bit later he cuts his foot with the hoe. Being in a hurry, however, he continues to work, getting more and more upset, and mad at himself that he has a cut. He comes inside, sees that he's late for his next engagement, looks at the cut, slaps a band-aid on it, and goes off. Now he's tense, anxious, and up-tight. He comes home, goes to sleep, and when he wakes up he feels a pain in his leg. He looks down and sees a big, puffy, red area, swollen and tender, with a little red streak running up his leg. Cursing his bad luck, he runs to the doctor to get some penicillin. This little story happens all the time in many different ways.

Here's how self-healing might have occurred. Imagine yourself being this person out in the garden. You're working hard and fast, and then you stub your toe. Now, that can be an early warning sign. Maybe you're working a little too fast, or you're a little upset, or your head is somewhere else. Whatever the warning sign might be, heed it. If it's stubbing your toe, or getting a little headache or cramp, right then is the time for clear observation. You might close your eyes and ask yourself what is going on.

But suppose you didn't do that, and instead you went on

to cut yourself with the hoe. At that point there is definitely something happening to the integrity of your body-mind-spirit. You now have an injury and it's very real. Now you stop for sure and ask, "What is happening?" If this were the freeway instead of the garden it might be when you've just had a close call and you're a little bit shaken. This is an extremely important place to stop and take a moment just to be with the situation. You've somehow injured yourself; it didn't happen by accident. Why? What is this about, what does it represent? You would realize that you weren't paying attention. You were doing one thing while thinking about another. You were tense, rushed, nervous, or distracted. Maybe this is a time to get a mental image about the injury. With your visualization you might see the cut as anxious, nervous energy expressing itself physically. You might see that what you need is to allow this energy to settle and be quiet for a while. This might lead you to slow down or to stop work in the garden. You might go inside and do something about the cut right then. Maybe you'd wash it out. Then you might sit down and notice that your foot feels better when it's propped up on a chair or stool. This takes some observation. It takes stopping to notice it. If you don't quiet down to listen you'll never notice what feels better and what feels worse.

Further along in the vignette, you might realize you've been rushing around all day, in fact all week. You've almost hurt yourself several times. You've lost your temper. Now you have a real injury. Perhaps what you need is not to go to the next engagement. So maybe you take it easy and stay home. You notice how the foot feels good raised up a bit, and how comfortable it feels when you wash it in warm water rather than cold. You might soak it again later that evening. You might even keep it up when you're asleep that night. Your body sends you all these messages, and you are able to hear them. And when you wake up the next morning, that cut is practically healed.

In fact, the healing would even more likely be complete

if, while you were resting in a relaxed yet focused state, you visualized the cut getting better. You might have seen the torn membranes coming together, watched healing new blood nourishing the area, observed some bacteria trying to get in but being smashed away by the antibodies. In short, you might have imagined the cut beginning to heal, getting better and better.

To do all this you must spend a few extra moments of quiet time. It's well worth it, because you benefit in several important ways. When you visualize the cut getting better you are actually facilitating the healing process by concentrating the healing energy in that part of the body. Also you are benefitting your entire system by being quiet and restful. Your nerves cool down. You become less agitated. Your system replenishes itself. A deep and fundamental healing of your whole being is taking place. Indeed, this has been time well spent.

An added chapter to this vignette has the first person going to the doctor, but coming home too preoccupied to follow his advice. The cut gets worse and worse, the infection spreads, until finally the leg has to be amputated. Or later he goes back into the garden and does the same thing, not learning from experience. But this time he's using a power tool and cuts his foot off entirely! This is not farfetched; many people go through this experience in one fashion or another. They get a distant early warning signal and they ignore it. Then they get a slightly stronger signal, perhaps a little injury, which they also ignore. Finally, since the more gentle messages didn't get through, they get really ill. Then they say, "How did this happen? What a stroke of bad luck!" when really it was the final stage of something they were continually doing to themselves.

Many people who have that fatal car crash have had lots of close calls beforehand. If you've been having some close calls, that's something for you to notice and to probe, perhaps via self-hypnosis. Lots of folks who have had major illnesses have had other warning signs along the way. They have had a little cold that didn't get better, but just dragged on and on. They have had cuts that didn't heal, poor digestion, frequent raw nerves, or numerous accidents. These are not necessarily symptoms of disease, but rather of poor general health.

Insurance companies and major firms have studied rather extensively the phenomenon of accident-prone individuals. Over a five-year period at a major auto plant, accidents happened to the same small group of people all the time, even at different places in the factory and at different jobs. If these accidents had been just random events they wouldn't have been happening to the same 10 percent of the people all the time. They were not random events or "accidents." There are no "accidents"; we attract events in accordance with our inner state. Accidents are messages from ourselves to ourselves. People who are accident-prone often admit to having had thoughts like, "I was thinking something like that would happen to me." This means such people helped make it happen, or participated in its happening, simply by imagining the accident. Similarly, people who are sick all the time contribute to their poor health with thoughts and images of illness. Hypochondriacs are people who give themselves a lot of negative suggestions and visualizations. They establish an unfortunate vicious circle: their negative attitude helps create illness, while their illness reinforces their negative attitude. We constantly involve ourselves in all aspects of our health, our well-being, our life in general. We can create or uncreate our accidents or illnesses.

Doctors may also contribute to illness when they approach their patients with a great deal of stress on the negative. We know of two equally competent urology surgeons at a large medical center who have very different results. One always encounters a lot of complications and side effects, the other hardly ever. They both try to prevent complications, but their styles have an important difference.

The first surgeon gives his patients largely negative

suggestions. For instance, he'll say to one of his patients the night before surgery (which is a very suggestible time), "When you wake up you'll have a tube in your bladder so the urine can come out. You'll notice there will be pain, because the bladder is trying to push the tube out; it's a foreign body, and it's red and raw and tender in there. . . ." The surgeon somehow figures this explanation will help the patient by preparing him for the worst. Sure enough, the patient wakes up the next morning and it's red and raw and tender. There's a lot of pain, and the nurse has to call the doctor because the tube has been expelled. Then they have to put in a new tube, and there are all sorts of complications.

The other doctor puts out a different feeling. The night before he'll say, "When you wake up in the morning, so you won't be surprised, you'll notice there will be a tube in your bladder. That tube is your friend. It's allowing the urine to come out without your having to make any effort at all; it's helping you out. The more you relax, the less you will notice it. It would stay there very nicely for a week or two, but we'll take it out in a couple of days." Complications for this surgeon are far more rare, because he doesn't lay it on thick. Laying it on thick ("Yes, there's a 20 percent chance of the bladder having to come out completely; there's a 10 percent chance of severe infection; and the anesthesia can kill you, of course") is bad medicine. Doctors who sow such negative seeds have more problems, and they can't understand why.

Take a lesson from these surgeons. Give yourself suggestions with positive language only. Rather than, "My nausea will stop," say, "I'm going to be thirsty and hungry." Rather than going to the doctor for a checkup with pictures of cancer or disease in your mind, focus on health. Think and talk about success and health. Watch to see when you talk about health if you don't sit up a little straighter, and perhaps breathe a little better. You are actually beginning to bring about health right then.

The previous examples illustrate the importance of following our three rules for self-healing. Now we will describe exactly how all this is used in a typical self-hypnosis session. Keep in mind that the following is only an example. The actual process may be much more detailed and specific. In addition, such details might vary from person to person and from problem to problem.

Choose the part of your body to be healed before going into self-hypnosis. Sit quietly and pay attention to that part of your body for a moment.

Begin by going through a basic self-hypnotic "induction process" as we have outlined earlier in this book. (Some people find it helpful to use a tape recorder. You can make a general tape for inducing trance. You can also make special tapes for whatever you want specifically to work on.) Once you are in self-hypnosis at a comfortable depth, begin to visualize clearly that part of your body that you have chosen for healing. (This can be a particular spot or organ, or an entire "system," such as the respiratory system.)

See the particular area you are healing clearly in your mind's eye. (See either its true anatomy or a symbolic representation of it, as discussed earlier.)

Now see that part of your body getting healthier, cleaner, clearer, stronger, more supple. See the healing process as it IS happening RIGHT NOW. Visualize the area becoming whole, healthy, and strong. See it happening RIGHT NOW.

This part of your body IS getting healthier, it IS getting cleaner, it IS getting stronger, RIGHT NOW, right before your mind's eye. See it getting better and better—feel it getting better and better.

Now as you concentrate on this healing process you may notice a very interesting and exciting thing begin to happen—ever so slightly at first, then stronger and stronger. As you concentrate on this process, you can begin to feel your body's natural healing forces rally to the spot. Energy starts migrating to the area you are healing, as if that part of your body has become somehow magnetic and is attracting positive force. All this positive healing energy begins to concentrate itself in that area of your body that you have chosen to be better. You feel it getting energized . . . getting warmer as more and more blood flows into the area. You may want to see it begin to glow as the healing energy is increased. You might see it surrounded by white or gold light.

With each breath you take, imagine that you are breathing *into* the area you are working on. Each breath brings more and more healing energy into the spot. This is healing energy from within and without, all directed to the place you are healing.

And YOU ARE HEALING . . . you see it and feel it and KNOW it is getting better and better—healthier and stronger RIGHT NOW as you concentrate.

After doing this healing process for about fifteen or twenty minutes, you can stop and come out of self-hypnosis as you have been taught earlier in this book . . . coming out slowly and comfortably. But, before you come out, tell yourself that this healing process that you have started is going to continue energizing and healing on its own until the next time you go into self-hypnosis. That next time is when you repeat and renew the process.

In between hypnosis sessions the process is continuing to work for you via "posthypnotic suggestion." This is one of the most powerful tools of self-hypnosis. It means that while in the process you make a suggestion that something will happen after the process is over. It is astounding but scientifically proven that these suggestions do get followed, even long after the hypnosis process is finished. Thus, the healing you initiate during the hypnosis process can continue on its own all day, if you suggest to yourself that this will happen.

We recommend that you do this healing "process" three times a day (along with any other treatment that you are doing) until the problem has cleared. Then do it once a day for a week or two, to be even more certain that the problem is completely resolved.

To sum up, then, we examined how to "heal ourselves," and how to allow the natural healing process to operate in us without obstruction. We saw the importance of clear observation, which means becoming aware of all the factors now operating in our lives. We also saw how many of these factors are frequently unconscious thoughts and images.

Next we learned to let these images go, replacing them with positive ones. The simple rule is to imagine things getting better.

Finally, we saw the importance of visualizing what we want to happen in as vivid and specific a fashion as possible. Being relaxed and focused in the hypnotic state provides us with great power, so that healing and health promotion can continually take place as a constant part of our daily lives.

9

Exploring Extra-Ordinary States

A generation ago the people in our culture who took an interest in extra-ordinary states of consciousness were few in number, and were considered by most to be a lunatic fringe. Times have changed. Today, many people have explored a different quality of consciousness. Their paths have been diverse: some have meditated, some have taken hallucinogens, some have pushed themselves beyond normal physical limits, some have deprived their senses. Others have come upon these new states quite spontaneously. Three questions immediately arise: What are extra-ordinary states of being? Can they be cultivated? Have they a place in our lives as we strive toward a healthier, more harmonious existence?

To answer the first question we need to take a broad look at the basic forces of energy in our world and how these energies function. The universe is energy in motion. This energy forms itself into patterns, vibrating at many different levels and rates called frequency. What we call "matter" is energy vibrating in a relatively slow, or gross frequency. Electromagnetic frequencies display themselves as light, as x-rays, as cosmic rays, etc. This is energy vibrating more rapidly than energy that we perceive as matter, although it is all one energy. Sound is energy. Thought is also energy, at a still finer frequency. All physical and psychic phenomena are ways energy has of forming patterns. And each person has a distinct limit within which he or she can perceive this energy. You may hear sounds between the frequency of 20 and 20,000 vibrations per second. A dog may hear a much higher frequency. Scientific instruments can be seen as extensions of our sensory apparatus that have greatly increased the realm in which we can perceive energy.

In our culture, we tend to accept as normal, or "ordinary," that which falls within the realm of our senses (extended by scientific instruments). We also tend to reject as superstition anything which falls outside this realm. But what if you could perceive energies which vibrate at a different rate from that which most people would perceive? You would then be a psychic or a mystic, either acknowledged as someone very special in some cultures, or dismissed as a madman in others. There are actually such people in every culture, people for whom the ordinary has extended to include states and powers beyond the experience of the majority. Some of these people are genetically endowed with these abilities. Others have worked on themselves over a period of time to increase their range of perception of the energies in the universe and to change their ways of relating to these energies.

Our beings give forth an energy which extends a certain distance beyond the body. This energy cannot be perceived by most people. Those who can perceive it have called it the "aura." Auras vary with the mood and the quality of consciousness of the individual. Science has dismissed auras in the West, but in Russia a new form of photography was developed which provides tangible evidence that auras exist as a natural phenomenon in nature. Kirlian photography has been an inspiration to explorers in the psychic realm, and an embarrassment to the old guard scientists of the West, whose foundations about what is "real" are being regularly shaken by increasing new evidence that supports scientifically what was once seen as only mystical and superstitious.

The more progressive scientists are beginning to agree (from a variety of perspectives) that energy behaves the same way whether it is operating at the cellular level or at the levels of solar systems and galaxies. Cells can do three basic things with energy: they can store it, they can transmit it, and they can reproduce themselves to do it again. Cells may group together in certain patterns to do all this more efficiently, but fundamentally that is all they do.

If you move to the planetary and galactic level to observe the way energy behaves you find the same three things: energy is stored, transmitted, and its patterns are reproduced, all according to the same basic laws of nature. Ancient wisdom noted this in the Hermetic maxim, "As above, so below." In practice, this means that we can learn about the universe by observing ourselves, and learn about ourselves by observing the universe. The greater our range of perception, the more we can learn.

So-called psychic phenomena are really nothing very special. The same laws of the universe are in operation. The ways of perceiving or relating to energy are simply being expanded. We have the ability to do this in our daily lives. In fact, we do it, but are often unconscious of its occurrence.

Let's take an example which has happened to almost everybody. You walk into a room full of people whom you don't know. Nobody has said anything, you haven't even gotten a chance to fully process what you see, but you can tell that something very heavy is going on. It is as if the air were charged with strong feelings. Now, how did you know this? Aside from visual clues such as facial expressions and postures, wasn't there something else, something which couldn't be reduced to anything coming in through the five senses? You picked up on a quality of intensity through a vibration which could be felt, but not in a way traditional science would have allowed as evidence. These incidents happen quite regularly.

In the normal so-called "waking" state our minds are usually filled with thoughts about the problems of our daily lives. This keeps us occupied at a certain level which desensitizes us to much of what is going on in and around us. During sleep, this surface, conscious layer is more dormant, which allows deeper layers to send forth their messages. Unresolved areas which can date back to early childhood may emerge, usually in highly symbolic ways. But because we are asleep we often fail to remember. And in sleep we have given up conscious control, so we are at the mercy of wherever these deeper states may take us.

Here lies the value of controlled alternate states of consciousness, ways of being that are neither awake in the ordinary sense, nor asleep. There remains a level of consciousness which can follow what is happening, take note for future reference, and integrate this material in our daily lives. There also is some sense of direction and control over what is happening. Yet the mind is free from the desensitizing sludge of daily consciousness which prevents deeper thoughts from surfacing. All psychic phenomena are in one way or another related to trance states. Whether it is healing, visions, precognition, seeing deeper into hidden levels of being, or whatever—the energy level of the normal state is too coarse to allow these more refined occurrences to take place. By involving oneself with self-hypnosis it is possible to begin to open the gate to these new levels of experience. These self-experience exercises become an integral part of spiritual growth. To keep the body well-tuned we have to exercise and maintain a proper diet. Seeing deeply into ourselves and our relationship with the world around us is a proper exercise and diet for the spirit.

Most of the psychic phenomena we read about involve some form of the self-hypnotic process. A "medium" will go into a trance, change the quality of her energy, and be able to tune into other entities the way a short wave radio can pick up finer frequencies. If she has precognition (the ability to see future events), she is changing her relationship with time. For us time is an incomplete experience of another dimension, limited by the quality of our minds. This limitation expresses itself as what seems to be a one-directional flow. When the limitation is dissolved through personal energy changes, a gap can open up in the time continuum which allows what we call the "future" to be seen in the present. From our perspective this is extraordinary; from a broadened perspective it is quite natural.

Healers also employ self-hypnosis. For the psychic healer or the tribal shaman to be successful, both he and the patient must be in an altered state of consciousness. The patient, often in pain or frightened, unable to deal with his energy the way it is, may revert naturally or with a minimum of suggestion to another mode of consciousness. This is a common occurrence in any kind of crisis. The healer is well experienced at changing his own state, realizing that a particular focus of energy, not possible in the ordinary state, is necessary for the healing to work. What is created is an energy exchange, a circular flow rather than the healer "doing something" to the patient. In this flow of energy the body's own amazing healing resources are mobilized. In such situations the "miraculous" can and often does occur.

Cultures more attuned than ours to the rhythms of life have recognized the importance of altered states of consciousness in the transition from one period of life to another. There are particular occasions in personal growth where it is apparent that one is leaving a particular mode of existence and entering into a new quality of experience. Adolescence is an example of such a time. Cultures like that of the American Indian have allowed in their structures a symbolic expression for making this transition. By their very nature these "rites of passage" are linked with a changed state of being. In some cultures teen-agers are encouraged to go into the wilds and invite the deeper parts of their being to become manifest, often as a vision. Altered states can be brought about through extreme physical exertion, through fasting, through certain exercises, through breathing, through sensory deprivation, and through many different self-hypnotic techniques, such as the repetition of a mantra. The visions which often result serve as a focus for the person's spiritual growth. The normal state is consciously altered so that spirituality may become an experienced, vital, living part of one's being rather than a set of beliefs about metaphysics. Thus religion infuses all the activities of one's daily life, rather than existing, as it does for so many, as a fragmented experience separate from the other aspects of living.

Western man, lacking the organized rituals for reaching extra-ordinary states, can still tap into these energies through self-hypnosis. We are going to show you several processes for getting in touch with deeper layers of your being. These are not to be played with lightly. The first two should not be done on a regular, frequent basis. Rather, they are to be used with seriousness and care at times when you feel the need for deeper guidance.

THE ROSE MEDITATION. People in widely different cultures have surprisingly similar images and symbols for the same deep, subconscious traits. One of the most widely consistent images is the rose, which everywhere symbolizes the emotional, nurturing aspect of our being. Psychic energies tend to pattern themselves so that there are places of great concentration of energy within the body. These places of concentrated energy are called "chakras." The rose is a universal symbol for the fifth, or heart chakra. This has been the case for the Egyptians, the Aztecs, the Greeks, and the American Indians as well as other cultures.

By focusing psychological energy on the symbol, the chakra is activated. This is not surprising when we consider how a person in financial difficulty will focus a great deal of thought energy on another symbol: money. Worrying about money can actually bring glandular and chemical changes to the body at the cellular level. Symbols allow for a convenient means of directing psychic energy, and the rose has been used as a symbol since ancient times in healing, meditative, and religious rites.

Doing the Rose Meditation is deceptively simple. You merely sit in a comfortable position, close your eyes, and visualize in front of you, as clearly as possible, a single rose. No special induction or deepening process is employed. You just observe the rose and let it do whatever it will. Don't put any demand on your mental functioning. The image may change, perhaps flowing into other images. Let it be, accept whatever comes up. Often this process will allow significant messages from the unconscious to emerge in symbolic form. These messages can be stepping stones to growth. Since they are at an emotional-spiritual level, you won't want to reduce them to the intellectual level by analyzing them, labeling them, categorizing them, and "figuring them out." These responses are almost automatic, but they detract from the quality of any deep and direct experience. So just let your rose tell its tale without interruption.

THE SPIRIT GUIDE PROCESS. Here is another technique whose profundity warrants the same suggestion to do it only at important times (periods of transition, or special occasions such as solstice). To do the process, put yourself into hypnosis. While in the state you suggest to yourself that on the other side of the transition plateau there is going to appear a being. This person will be there for you when you go through the door, the fog, across the bridge, or whatever symbol you have chosen. You don't know who this person will be. It may be someone you've never seen, or someone from your past, alive or dead, someone you've heard of, or it may even be yourself, either at your present age or a lot older. The person may appear very clearly, or may be hazy and indistinct.

Whatever form the image of the person takes, you go up to it and ask a question related to your growth and development. The image may give you a perfectly comprehensible answer, it may say words which don't make any sense to you, or it may just remain silent. You accept whatever happens without having a discussion or a debate about the answer. At this point you may wish to remain quiet for a period, or you can return to your normal state.

Who or what is this being that has appeared to give forth its wisdom? Is it a mere figment of your imagination? Does it come from within you or from some external source? We know for sure that this process works, that the image which appears can give truly profound and appropriate advice, but it is not for us to give any kind of final word on the origin of the image. One strong possibility involves parts of consciousness residing in us. Primal, wise, and sensitive in nature, these aspects of our being get drowned out by the usual noise of our internal monologue. When this noise is silenced and the appropriate suggestions are given, these deeper aspects of consciousness may take a form suitable to our understanding, perhaps based on our own unique way of symbolizing things.

At the most profound levels of consciousness the boundaries between ourselves and the rest of the universe may not be as absolute as the conscious mind likes to believe. Therefore, at these levels it is not even meaningful to make a distinction between what is in us and what is outside of us. All we can say for sure is that some kind of wisdom is in operation. And since there isn't a great deal of wisdom about, it makes sense to be able to plug into what is available. Again, we suggest that you have a question in mind before you start, and don't do this process casually or too often.

If you are like many people in our Western culture you tend to analyze things, compare them, label them, and judge them. While this is obviously necessary for certain levels of daily existence, it can be overdone to the detriment of another, more direct way of being and learning. Trying to understand things rationally can frequently block deeper forms of understanding. You don't have to analyze a sunset! The same principle applies to the Spirit Guide Process that applies to the Rose Process: let the message seep into your being, and be still with it. It will produce its own action in your life far more effectively if you simply accept it, rather than if you rake it over with the finetoothed cleverness of your rational mind.

Psychics are in common agreement that Western man has two fundamental problems. The first we have just mentioned: the overdeveloped rational mind. The second is a lack of groundedness. Our culture encourages us to go through the day and through the entire seasonal progression in minimal contact with the earth which we live on and which supports us. To be in direct contact with the earth involves seeing oneself and one's relationships from a different perspective. It means to be more centered, and to feel oneself as a part of something greater, not just intellectually but at the core of one's being. The following process will help you get in touch with the energy of the earth.

THE GROUNDING PROCESS. Sit erect, close your eyes, and focus your attention on the area at the base of the spine. This is the first chakra, a powerful concentration of energies whose focus lies in the realm of basic survival needs and raw, primitive energies. Feel all your energy centering at the first chakra. At the same time feel your feet relax and open up so that they allow more energy to flow through them. Each time you exhale feel that you are pumping your breath powerfully down through the legs, out the feet, into the earth, and right down to its center. Each time you inhale feel yourself drawing in the deep, primal energy of the earth, and feel it filling your whole being. Continue as long as you wish. Of course it makes sense to do this one out-of-doors. With practice you may experience a new quality of awareness whenever you take a walk or just sit under a tree.

This quality, a communion with what is around us, is increasingly necessary if we are to survive on this planet. For example, in some very basic way there is a relationship between what cancer cells do to the body and what our species is doing to the earth. Cancer cells can store energy, but have lost the ability to transmit it. And because of this they lose the ability to communicate with the cells around them. Therefore they no longer take into account the needs of that which surrounds them, and they begin proliferating indiscriminately, destroying the delicate balance in the rest of the body. This means that they also destroy themselves, for when the body can no longer function, the cancer cells have lost their source of nourishment. We seem to be doing the same thing on this planet. Our fate may well be the fate of the cancer cells unless we learn to be in a different, more integrated relationship with the world around us. The next process, along with the previous one, can help bring this about.

THE ENERGY EXCHANGE PROCESS. Sit in front of a plant, a tree, or anything that you feel has life (for some this will include rocks, mountains, etc.). Assuming you've chosen a plant, center yourself for a while, and then begin to imagine a beam of energy flowing between the plant and you (close your eyes and continue to feel this beam of energy). Then visualize that your knowing self, your essence, some of the very stuff that is you, rides that beam out of your body and into the plant. The same beam sends back some of the freshness, the essence of the plant, and you welcome it into your being. An energy exchange has come into being, a circular flow, an intermingling of essences.

Many primitive people, herbalists, and other true lovers of nature are relating with plants in a manner similar to this. The herbalist may find that the plant will give forth its message, and inform him of its uses and benefits. American Indians would relate to a plant before picking it for food, and before taking it into their system. There is more than beauty in this gesture: it leads to greater health. In such a state it is considerably harder to take in harmful chemicals. How much more intimately can you relate to your environment than by eating? The essence of what you take in becomes part of you at a cellular level. It is as though the earth is an organism and you are one of its cells. These processes can put you in touch with interconnectedness at all levels of being. And that is, in fact, the true meaning of spirituality.

We would like to remind you of one important distinction between processes in former chapters (healing, stress reduction, etc.) and the spiritual meditations given here. In the former you dictate. You suggest that a particular thing is going to happen, and your focus helps to bring it about. In spiritual meditations you are just open for whatever comes. The more open you are, the less you dictate, the less you are trying to control. You are not even trying rationally to understand anything. You are open, like an empty vessel. The more open you are, the more will come to you. The less you force yourself to understand, the more you will know.

IV

A Key Tool for Total Health

10

Waking Up to Ourselves

At this point we would like to describe to you what we mean by "total well-being" and how self-hypnosis helps achieve it. For a firm foundation of good health all three aspects of our being—physical, mental, spiritual—must be developed to their full potential. The basic tenet of holistic philosophy is that true and lasting health is of the whole self. All the parts of our being are so completely interrelated that if one part is not functioning well, the total efficiency of the system is destroyed. Imagine a car with a fine, well-tuned engine, a good body and tires, but with a faulty transmission. No one would want to drive such a car; yet, analogously, this often tends to be the state of our health.

Consider a more graphic illustration. Picture a horizontal line representing the entire spectrum between illness and wellness, with health increasing as you move to the right. Premature death would then be at the far left end. Just to the right of that lies serious illness and major disability. Still farther to the right we encounter minor illness and disability, then various symptoms, such as aches and pains, continuous low energy, frequent depression, and bad digestion. Even farther to the right are signs which you may not even be aware of but that a trained specialist could detect.

An example of these would be too many white corpuscles in the bloodstream. Eventually we reach a place on the line far enough to the right so that all illness, disease, symptoms, and more subtle signs have vanished. Is this health? Is health simply the absence of disease?

According to our conditioning it is. For many people the line ends here. This completes the area which has been so thoroughly investigated by Western medicine. If we simply assume that freedom from illness means good health, we are totally neglecting what may lie farther to the right. There lies the domain of holistic health, and the beginning of an exciting investigation of more total well-being.

As we move more to the right along the continuum we begin to taste for ourselves that state of being which may be called positive wellness. This hasn't been studied very much; its stages are not familiar territory for most Western scientists, doctors, and psychologists. How does positive wellness differ from mere absence of disease?

The feeling from within is the major difference. The simple fact of being a living person has a positive, bounteous quality to it. There is a feeling of aliveness and abundance of energy which may go into creativity and into keeping the organism free of ills. There is a harmony, both with one's environment and within oneself. There is an appropriateness to one's actions. A general feeling of vitality and well-being is unmistakably projected.

Individual aspects of high level wellness are just now starting to be investigated and tested. In the realm of physical fitness there are tests which measure how much air people can move in and out of their lungs and how long it takes the heart to recover normal speed after various types of stress. The results for a truly well person may differ considerably from those for a "normal" person, one who is at the midpoint in the spectrum. There are also certain psychological tests which measure the degree of self-actualization or positive functioning. These are different from tests which measure pathology, illness, and neurotic behavior. Much of what is called the Human Potential Movement involves methods to explore and create circumstances for staying on the right side of the midpoint. High level wellness is not a goal. It is a by-product, a natural outcome of becoming familiar with the effects that different lifestyles have on your health. By then choosing activities which are beneficial to your well-being you move to the right on the line. Since we are always learning, never static, wellness becomes an ongoing process, a way of life rather than a place which we reach.

Each of the three aspects—physical, mental, and spiritual—is totally necessary for wellness. The physical is the most obvious. One can't be truly well without a vital, smoothly functioning machine. Mentally, there must be a limit to unnecessary stress, for stress is one of the major factors in illness. Psychological well-being also includes having healthy personal relationships, an ability to communicate emotions, and genuinely liking oneself. An absence of repressed feelings is essential. Negative feelings which are not dealt with consciously and directly can act like a psychological cancer, causing great damage to one's health.

The hidden health factor is often the spiritual aspect. A surprising number of people reach their middle years with their bodies, relationships, and jobs reasonably intact. Nothing visible seems wrong with their lives, and yet a voice begins to make itself heard that something is missing. "Is this all there is?" is a frequent expression of an emptiness on the spiritual plane. And when things are not right here, there can be no real health.

What is the spiritual plane? Is it belonging to some religion? Is it talking or thinking a great deal about philosophy and God? Not necessarily. In simplest terms, to be spiritual is to be "related." The factor which prevents our natural spirituality from exhibiting itself in our lives is isolation. To be spiritual is to be conscious of our relationship to our environment, to our fellow humans, to nature, and to that which lies beyond the world of the senses. Our connectedness is always a fact at every instant. But our *awareness* of connectedness may have become coated over in our battle to survive as individuals. As we get older we tend to put more and more energy into protecting our own little world, which may be seen as a process of isolating ourselves. We do our best to get comfortably isolated and secure. Sometimes no amount of belief, thought, or words can pierce that isolation.

That isolation *is* the feeling that something is missing. Experiencing a vacuum, we try to fill the emptiness with different kinds of pleasure. Not really knowing what we want, we throw ourselves into the accumulation of money and possessions, we take drugs, we demand endless entertainment, all in the hope of filling this vacuum. The more frantically we try to fill it the more unsatisfied we feel. Here, indeed, is the hidden health factor. When one is interested in philosophical or spiritual matters and explores them, there begins to come about a feeling of connection, a lessening of isolation. Whatever happens in living is experienced in a new context, the context of a whole which gives it meaning. To feel connectedness and deep meaning in what one does is essential for aliveness and true, holistic health. But more about that at the end of this chapter.

Our health is a most sensitive reflection of how our overall life is working. Wellness is not achieved by merely superimposing a few "healthy" activities onto a typical frantic, unhealthy lifestyle. There are those who gorge themselves all day with junk food, but then soothe their conscience with a vitamin pill and a dose of sprouts. The body is not fooled; its health is an extremely accurate barometer of how well it is being treated. It not only reflects the quality of diet, but also of what might be called "Total Diet." This includes not only food, drink, and drugs, but also the air breathed, and even the sense impressions taken in. Those who go from working in a noisy factory by day to a crowded, smoke-filled bar by night are partaking of a diet that may lead to ill health just as inevitably as if they ate only junk food. To get out from time to time into nature may well be an essential ingredient of one's Total Diet. Food, air, and sense impressions get taken in, digested, and in some way become part of us. It is easy to assess the quality of these, and to see their effect on our long-range health.

Thus, it's a good idea to look at our activities and see if the health-giving ones are an integrated part of our daily living, rather than something thrown in on top of an un-healthy lifestyle. The kind of activities that lead to health grow from understanding and appreciation rather than from a grim sense of duty. If, for example, you get up and jog out of sheer willpower and obligation, it is questionable whether you are doing yourself any good. Therefore the question arises, how can wholeness and harmony be achieved in a natural, organic, unforced way?

Each of the three aspects we have mentioned—physical, mental, and spiritual—can be developed to its optimum, if there is interest. Developing something to its optimum often involves finding out areas of weakness and giving them special attention. For example, within the physical you might know already whether your diet or exercising is of high caliber, and if not you might want to motivate yourself (perhaps with hypnosis—but we'll come to that soon) to do something about it.

With many people one of the major problems is that their lives resemble a tripod with one short leg, unbalanced and ready to topple over. The short leg can be the body, the mind, or the spirit. Everyone has a different makeup; and you can discover the weakest aspect of your being if you become interested in creating balance, in equalizing the legs of your tripod. Many people avoid some part of them-selves. Avoidance leads to stagnation, and the person will say, "I'm not interested in any of those health food ideas," or, "All that philosophy stuff just isn't for me." The very areas of our being that we avoid are most often our weakest links. A person might be highly spiritually oriented, eat the right food and get the right exercise, but have very poor-quality relationships. Another might have good relation-ships and be smothering himself under a layer of fat. Whatever your least-developed aspect, you can promote balance by giving it new interest or added attention. There are many interesting books out now on all three aspects, and sometimes a bit of reading will give a few clues on how to proceed.

THE WEAKEST LINK PROCESS can help you sense more clearly what aspect or aspects of your life are most in need of attention in order to bring about more balance. You simply place yourself into a hypnotic state, and give yourself the suggestion that a wise person, a sage, a personal teacher, a guru, or any other similar figure, comfortable to you, will appear as you go through the door, the fog, etc. This may be your spirit guide, or someone you imagine in advance. Ask your wise mentor these questions: "Is there any area of my being it would be appropriate to work on at this point in my life? How might I go about it?" You may or may not get a useful reply. Or perhaps the answer may not come to you at that time, but later in a flash of intuition or understanding. If you don't understand the answer, just live with it for a while and see what happens.

Of course, the real excitement and newness happen when you begin to grow within all three dimensions at once, experiencing more and more their interrelationship. For example, the more sensitive you become to your body, the more you'll see how the little fluctuations in its hourly chemistry have a remarkably powerful effect on your psy-chological state. None of these aspects of yourself is a separate fragment. Each reflects the whole and this affects the whole. The more conscious you become of this interrela-tionship, the healthier you will be. And then the same activities will have significance for you on two or three levels at once. Some activities lend themselves particularly well to combining.

For example, suppose that you need to go to work and that you need exercise. It may be possible for you to jog or bicycle to work. In this way, the needed exercise becomes a useful integral part of your life. Or you might try out an activity such as gardening. The physical labor can help keep you in shape. The quiet, relaxing nature of the work can ease your tension. And the nurturing and caring for living things can awaken a sense of participation in something larger, a connectedness with the earth.

Another activity particularly suited to combining is Yoga. The postures are a superb tonic for the whole body. The mind becomes less agitated, more alert and centered. And from this quietness one can touch into deeper spiritual levels of being.

Hiking with a friend is another way of bringing health simultaneously at different levels. A vigorous walk in a lovely place is good for the body and soul. Sharing a relaxed and unstructured time with a friend can have a mellowing effect on one's state. And such a setting can frequently inspire moments of inner grandeur, which sometimes require a bit more space than daily life usually offers.

What we have been doing is painting a broad picture, one whose details you can fill in as you explore ways in your own life to move to the right on your health line, towards high level wellness. Along the way you can make creative use of self-hypnosis in each of the three aspects, and in combining them.

You can begin by motivating yourself. Almost all of us have areas in our lives that we'd like to change. Sometimes we go for months or years, stuck with wanting to change, but never seeming to get off the ground. A push is needed; self-hypnosis can be that push.

Let's say you want to change your eating habits. You can begin in the hypnotic state to envision yourself choosing better food and not eating so much at night. Or if you feel it would be good to start some project, you can imagine yourself beginning to do and enjoy it. The focused awareness of self-hypnosis might get you off the ground far more efficiently than unreliable and erratic "willpower."

We've already mentioned how hypnosis can help you ascertain which areas are the weakest and most in need of attention. You can follow this up by learning to combine all three aspects in a very powerful way.

THE MEDITATIVE WALK PROCESS can touch you deeply on several levels. Find a time when you are free to take an unhurried walk. A rural area or a park would be nice, but anywhere is fine. Before the walk put yourself into a hypnotic state and give yourself the following suggestion, using any words that feel comfortable:

"I am going to go for a walk when I leave the hypnotic state. This will be very different from an ordinary walk. A new sensitivity will come upon me. I will be very receptive to lighting, color, shapes, and forms. I'll hear the sounds around me far more clearly. I'll smell all the subtle smells that I usually miss. I'll feel my body in all its variety of movement as it walks along, experiencing fully the animal that is me. I'll notice the clouds, the wind, and the birds. My mind will be quiet, alert, and relaxed. I won't concern myself with the details of my daily life. I'll let them go for the duration of the stroll; there will be plenty of time for that later. My mind will just remain with whatever is happening. I'll be interested in everything, and I'll pass judgment on nothing. I'll be relaxed, and thoroughly enjoy the total experience. I'll feel my relationship with the people I meet, the trees and plants I see, the earth, with everything. I will feel a total and comforting connectedness with my entire environment as I walk, and this will make me feel centered and good. There will be nothing I need to resist; I'll be at peace with the universe during this walk. And when I'm through, I will feel like I've been recharged, glad to reenter my daily life."

You can sense the benefit of learning how to respond to

your surroundings from this perspective. It is health-giving to you because you are being fully alive and exchanging energies harmoniously with your environment. It benefits the environment because you are more sensitive and your responses are likely to be more appropriate. In any of your hypnotic sessions you can include a suggestion about this perspective whenever you feel its lack is creating problems in your life.

To view the universe in this way feels immediately freeing. In a sense, moving towards greater wellness is at the same time moving towards freedom, away from being bound and restricted. This freedom manifests itself on each of the three aspects of being. On the physical plane, for example, there can arise a freedom from the many intrusions of the body, which prevent us from enjoying or even participating fully in our daily activity. Many people have lives relatively filled with headaches, stomach trouble, menstrual trouble, low energy, backache, infections, discomforts, and illnesses. To explore the right-hand side of the health spectrum, the well side, is to become more and more free of these intrusions, and be able to function at full capacity most of the time. That doesn't rule out ever getting sick but it does imply an ability to bounce back quickly, a sign of true health.

Freedom on the psychological plane does not, as some people think, mean freedom from all negative or unpleasant feelings. It does mean freedom from getting stuck in a particular negative attitude, feeling, or state. There is a natural flow to the rhythm of life, and the inevitable ups and downs are part of that rhythm. Negative feelings, when seen, acknowledged consciously, and given room to exist, get transformed with relative speed. Negative feelings which are unacknowledged, unconscious, and resisted, take root and remain as a constant presence, reappearing in various forms. Psychological freedom includes the attitude that whatever feeling is being experienced is best allowed rather than fought. Not fighting one's emotions or one's current state of mind gives one the freedom to act more fully and effectively in the world. Freedom from confusion, the ultimate psychological freedom, will begin to come about naturally in understanding more and more how we work.

There is no defined border as we move from the psychological to the spiritual. In fact, to examine the psychological thoroughly is to touch on the very essence of the spiritual. Exploring, for instance, the attachment we have to our ego begins to bring freedom from a major source of our dis-comfort and dis-ease. For example, it is in the nature of things as living creatures that we have our tastes, our preferences, our choices about the way we want things to be. Somewhere along the way we have picked up the strong tendency to give an ultimate value to these tastes and preferences and to identify our whole being with them (ego). Hence we make ourselves miserable much of the time, whenever things are not going according to our choices. This way of making ourselves miserable is an intrusion into the spirit. Greater wellness on the spiritual plane means freedom from these intrusions. Such freedom displays itself as a change in perspective to the events in one's life. The same preferences, the same reactions, the same feelings of good and bad now have underneath all of them a deeper feeling that whatever is happening is all right just the way it is, including perhaps our not liking it. When this occurs, our constant need to control our environment is greatly lessened, which brings an ease and grace to our lives. Another way of saying this is that freedom is to be less attached to things turning out a certain way. This happens gradually as we gain wisdom, and sometimes instantly at moments of clear understanding.

Moving in these ways towards greater and greater freedom in all aspects of our being, we derive a special bonus. We promote the well-being of humanity in general by creatively enhancing our own health. A healthy human being puts out a certain feeling that communicates itself at all levels to others. Everything we do touches other people in a way determined by the quality of our own wellness. By being healthy we set an example, we project a feeling of harmony and sanity into a world which sorely needs it.

Ill health is alienation and isolation; health is connectedness. The more clearly we see how this works, the more our boundaries can expand. Fundamentally, everything and everyone is related. We are all part of spaceship Earth. In looking at it this way, it's not that we lose our self-identity, but rather than the "self" we care about expands. First, this expansion may extend to include one's spouse as a part of oneself. Next, one's concept of self may expand to include one's family. Then it may expand further to include the community, the nation, the whole ecosystem, and finally all that is life. The truly healthy self-centered person will display a great deal of care towards herself and towards the rest of the world. On the other hand, war and pollution seem to stem from a lack of care for anything lying outside the small limiting boundaries we generally create for ourselves. Health involves care, and care means a transformed relationship to the earth and to its inhabitants. Ecological and social awareness are a natural by-product of waking up to ourselves.

Although we are totally connected with everything else, it sometimes helps if we can be reminded of that fact. Merely saying this to our intellect has little impact. The hypnotic state, however, may allow us to *feel* the actual fact of connectedness rather than have just a verbal assertion of it. The following process is one you can use any time you'd like to feel more connected to the rest of the universe.

BEING PART OF IT ALL PROCESS. Sitting comfortably in the hypnotic state, focus your attention on your body. Picture yourself getting smaller and smaller, so that you can experience the complex interactions of the atomic world. Picture a whole universe of atoms and molecules, and realize that you are part of all of that. Then shift your consciousness to the level of organs, chemical reactions, digestion, circulation, and feel how that is you and you are that. Expanding consciousness further, become aware of your immediate environment, with the plants, trees, animals, and people, feeling an important part of all. Dwell on each of these levels for a period before moving on. Keep expanding, feel other people in different parts of the world, leading different lives, but with the same basic feelings as you, and feel part of the whole global population. Then see the whole earth with everything on it and in it, and feel part of that. Finally, continue to expand as far out as your mind will allow you. Include the solar system, the galaxy, and finally all of creation. You *are* a part of all that, and what you are learning all the time is to dissolve the self-created barriers which make us seem to be separate. This is true waking up to one's self.

II

Putting Ourselves in Our Own Hands

The more one looks closely at the subtle workings of our beings the more impressive they seem. One of the most imposing aspects of our body-mind system is the existence of a directing inner wisdom. Emerging out of the deepest layers of our consciousness, this intelligence knows how to oversee our functioning so as to heal any dis-ease of the system, as well as to maintain the rest at optimal levels. It is a health-oriented inner wisdom, a major part of our legacy from simpler forms of life.

This inner wisdom, pervading our entire being, is a natural part of both the psychological and the physical planes. It makes up the very fabric of our body. Each cell expresses it, as well as the glands, organs, organ systems, and brain. The unerring force helps to heal cuts, digest food, protect the body from without and within, and regulate the internal chemistry. Its workings, mostly deep and unconscious, seem always to be helping the body recreate itself healthily.

The same phenomenon expresses itself somewhat differently on the psychological plane. Arising from depths far beneath the conscious mind, it is a wise counselor with a comprehensive understanding of ourselves and a profound vision of our environment. What we call "intuition" has this wisdom for a source. It participates in the healing of psychological dis-ease, such as depression. Just as it knows how to digest a meal, it knows how to heal the wounds caused by losing a loved one.

Although the inner wisdom is never-ceasing in its operation, we tend for the most part to be unaware of its workings. On the physical level, the body does most of its job better when the intellect doesn't interfere. Therefore on this level we are not conscious of the wisdom. Psychologically, what prevents our awareness of the wisdom is first that we get caught up by our daily concerns, running them over and over in our minds, thus losing the quiet inner environment necessary to hear subtle, refined messages. Second, we haven't been educated in a society which has recognized the existence and importance of inner wisdom. Therefore we haven't learned what to look for or how to listen.

Certain individuals and other whole cultures have recognized and named what we are describing. One such name has been the "Ghost within the Machine." This refers to the mysterious and invisible nature of this force which directs us from within, this spark of life for our mechanical body.

Another descriptive name has been the "Vital Force." Behind the scenes in our life processes can be found this basic drive, which organizes and balances inner processes. The Vital Force was believed at one point to have its own intelligence, a mind that was somehow separate from the mind of the individual.

Western scientists would never allow into their thinking such a mysterious concept of an unseen force which defied all their structures. What they were able to understand was the observable phenomenon of how our internal systems always tended towards a state of chemical balance, or equilibrium. For example, the body manages to regulate its own temperature within narrow limits. Acid-base balance, digestion, and oxygen consumption are all regulated in a finely tuned fashion, without conscious awareness having any understanding or knowledge of it. Therefore scientists coined the word "homeostasis," which means to stay the same. This was an acceptable scientific alternative to the more mystical descriptions of the same basic phenomenon. The scientists saw it as the ability of the organism to run on automatic. This is true enough, although it misses some of the deeper ways this wisdom can display itself.

Nobel Prize winner Albert Szent-Györgyi saw the wisdom as, "The drive in living matter to perfect itself." He observed how all units of life, from the single cell to a whole person, had a natural drive towards more perfect internal functioning and also towards a more harmonious relationship with the rest of the world. A unit of life can be a species, and Darwin discovered that over the course of many generations a species would become more and more in tune with its environment, perfecting itself in the process. The force that drives the cell, the individual animal, and the species is the same. Thus, evolution takes place in the individual as well as in the species, and the inner wisdom, or drive to perfection, is the means of this evolution, or movement towards health.

A more recent name for the internal wisdom is the "Two-Billion-Year-Old Healer." The knowledge of preventing and treating illness is the refined product of two billion years' worth of trial and error, originating with the dawn of life. These refinements are the source of our sophisticated equipment such as various systems which fight infection. Certain blood cells gobble up bacteria. Glands secrete in harmony to create the perfect chemical environment for rapid healing. The immune system produces proteins which bind up invading viruses. The result is that in each one of us is actually a wise, old healer, treating every kind of dis-ease, and knowing in any circumstances what is healthiest for us. Colds, stomachaches, cuts, sprains, all heal themselves. The psychological illness called depression usually heals itself in six to eight months, regardless of the medical or psychiatric treatment involved.

We can see that all of these different names—the "Inner Wisdom," the "Ghost within the Machine," the "Vital Force," "Homeostasis," the "Drive in Living Matter to Perfect Itself," and the "Two-Billion-Year-Old Healer"— all are pointing towards a single process, the existence of our health-oriented inner wisdom.

Although the inner wisdom is operating within us all the time, whether or not we are aware of it, part of the evolution towards health and perfection is to become more conscious of its messages and to utilize them more effectively. If you consider that this inner wisdom is part of the subconscious, and recall what an effective tool self-hypnosis can be for exploring deeper layers of the mind, then you will see what a royal road to inner wisdom self-hypnosis can be. We can employ self-hypnosis to be in touch with our most basic needs and drives, our most inner thoughts and feelings. The inner wisdom will speak to us and guide us, especially if we listen closely. There is no better way to listen closely than to put oneself in a state of self-hypnosis, sensitive and receptive. Then one can be receptive to all those subtle messages: the minor, fleeting emotions, the unconscious resistance, the initially gentle feedback of the body, the quality of digestion, and the deeper spiritual struggles which, at one level or another, are going on all the time, but are seldom experienced or observed directly. Self-hypnosis will enable us to tap into the inner wisdom and to utilize it more and more.

One of the ways the wisdom expresses itself is in what we have called the "Will to Live." Often people have nothing organically wrong with them, and yet their lives slip away simply because they feel there is no reason for them to live. The reverse can be seen in those who recover from serious illness when doctors offered little hope. Such people generally have an enormous will to live, stronger than any disease.

When we take a closer look at this principle, we see that it operates all the time, in ordinary daily life as well as in life-threatening illness. Therefore it should more properly be called the "Will to Be Well," since wellness is life expressing itself most completely ("whole" and "healthy" come from the same root). The state of our health depends to a very great extent on this facet of our inner wisdom. The will to be well is present in all of us, but it can be overshadowed, negated, or ignored by the conscious mind. The desire for immediate gratification sometimes runs counter to what is best for health, particularly when indulged in regularly and indiscriminately. The force of habit and conditioning may also oppose the will to be well, as when we get into the rut of eating, smoking, or drinking too much, or when we neglect proper exercise and relaxation. Feelings like fear, resentment, and despair may cloud the relationship we have with our inner wisdom, and prevent us from experiencing its message. Tension and fatigue may also set up a barrier which prevents some of our maintenance and surveillance mechanisms from operating.

Whether we are healthy or ill depends on this vital balance. Recovery from an illness has basically more to do with a healthy attitude than with the intervention of outside forces such as doctors, drugs, or healers. In fact, the whole fabric of health is directly tied into the daily operation of the will to be well. Therefore it is of utmost importance to acknowledge it and act on its messages.

Developing this will to be well means not only choosing more health-giving activities, but also choosing more positive attitudes. At any moment we can choose to withdraw energy from negative thoughts and to focus on the positive aspects of life. This actually promotes healing and encourages the prevention of illness. When we are psychologically relaxed the muscles also get relaxed. Blood is able to flow more freely into areas that require regeneration and repair. Revitalization begins to occur. So the more we allow and encourage positive attitudes the more we are developing in ourselves the will to be well. As we foster and bring into play our own internal healing abilities it becomes increasingly easy for these mechanisms to work for us.

Of course, it is necessary for the conscious mind to lend its support to the unconscious healing mechanisms, so that messages can be acted on rapidly and efficiently. To return to one of our favorite examples, if you cut yourself the internal wisdom knows well how to heal the cut, but healing is difficult if the wound has dirt in it. Therefore, the conscious self has to see that the wound is clean, to set the stage for optimal healing. The inner wisdom might also send messages regarding future behavior. In this case the message might be to be more alert and careful when using knives. The cut finger, like the near miss on the highway, can be a subtle but important indication to slow one's pace. If the conscious mind ignores such messages, as it frequently does, then the inner wisdom must send communications of a more jolting, serious nature, messages which are much harder to ignore. Many people have a whole series of minor accidents or close calls before actually having a major accident. Acting on the message is as important as hearing its content.

It's easier to pull out young, tiny weeds than to struggle with large, firmly rooted ones. This is true whether the weeds be accident or illness. Just as almost cutting a finger is a distinct message, so also is almost getting sick. A slightly scratchy throat, a runny nose, a mildly upset stomach can all be pointers to the beginning of imbalance in the system, easy to correct when caught at this early stage. When you learn how to listen, the inner wisdom can tell you the nature of the imbalance: perhaps you've been working and/or playing too hard; or perhaps you have some unresolved emotional problem. Head colds frequently begin directly after emotional encounters in which emotions have been suppressed. Whatever its nature, the imbalance is subject to easy correction when the inner wisdom tells you its nature, and the will to be well stimulates your alertness to the appropriate conscious action.

As we begin to refine our inner perceptions, we can become sensitive to even more subtle messages. We don't have to wait for the beginnings of colds, minor accidents, or near misses to detect the very first, delicate signs of imbalance in the system. Sometimes just quietly tuning into the state of your energy will give a vague feeling that something isn't quite right. Perhaps we might notice a slight irritability, somewhat low energy, or a mild touch of agitation or restlessness. To a sensitive, health-oriented person who employs self-hypnosis as a tool, most of the corrective work, most of the weeding, takes place at this subtle level before any symptoms actually occur.

We are going to explore how self-hypnosis can help us to contact the inner wisdom, to be guided and directed by it. To do this, some faith is required in this deep intelligence, or some direct experience of it. Several pieces of our conditioning, however, make it harder for this to happen. The first centers around the way we have been taught to conceive of ourselves as an "I," or ego. Modern science has recently rediscovered what the ancients knew—that our conscious mind is but a miniscule part of our total consciousness and that there is unfathomable depth and richness beneath the conscious layers. Our conditioning is to believe we are nothing but this small conscious layer, a separate entity, cut off from the rest of the universe by a barrier. This entity, or ego, is afraid of coming to an end, and therefore afraid of so many things in daily life that it constantly tightens itself, makes itself sick, and cuts itself off from the very wisdom in which can be found its salvation. It is sometimes hard for the conscious mind to let go sufficiently of its beliefs and struggles to allow other layers the opportunity for expression.

A second piece of conditioning makes it harder to have faith in ourselves. As a society we have an almost total dependence on the external manipulations of technology. Not only do we have the highest regard for machines, but we also trust medicines, pills, and surgical procedures to an inordinate degree as a means of health. We depend heavily on doctors and psychiatrists. Instead of assuming the responsibility for our own state, which is the mark of an adult, we have remained children in trusting the most intimate aspects of our being to something external. Instead of acting from self-knowledge, we have become a nation of patients, totally dependent on health professionals telling us what to do. This is not fertile soil for the inner wisdom to flower. We need, besides the tool of self-hypnosis, a total response to the wisdom. The passive part of our response is to trust its working, and to listen quietly to its message without interference from the fixed, opinionated, rational mind. The active part consists of heeding its message and acting on it when necessary, being willing to drop old ways of being.

With this distinction between passive and active contact, now we are ready for using self-hypnosis to get in touch with the inner wisdom. The initial stage will deal with the passive, listening aspect:

THE INNER WISDOM PROCESS—PASSIVE LISTENING. Once you are in the self-hypnotic state, remain quietly for a few minutes in your transition plateau. Then give yourself the following suggestion: "I understand the nature of the inner wisdom, always working for my greater health, and always willing to communicate to my conscious mind what is best for the organism. I understand that I need to trust its working, and to be receptive, to hear its message. When I come out of hypnosis there will be a new part of me, operating just below the conscious level, highly tuned to the messages of the inner wisdom. At periods during the day my conscious mind will become spontaneously quiet, and the conscious mind will receive messages which are appropriate. I will trust these messages, for they come from a place in me which is concerned for my deepest well-being."

As you tune in more and more you will see the importance of responding to positive feelings as well as negative ones. We put plenty of energy into avoiding those things which give us pain. Now we can begin to discover what positive feedback is, that particular sense of vitality and well-being in which our organism sends itself the message, "Whatever it is you're doing, do more of it!" In a spirit of inquiry, you can begin trying new activities, or stopping old, harmful ones. Sometimes the positive feedback can be overwhelming. The movement towards health involves experimenting with your lifestyle, listening to the feedback, and attempting more and more to do those things which bring on this feeling of well-being. In fact, this feeling is actually the beginning of good health.

Another insight from tuning into ourselves is the realization of our own uniqueness. External aid is usually based on generalized recommendations, not molded and modified to our own peculiar needs. Like a very cheap suit, it somewhat fits, but totally lacks that quality possessed by something carefully fitted to our exact measurements. Each individual has specific likes, dislikes, nutritional needs, personality structure, and patterns of conditioning and tightness. What is suitable exercise or diet for one may be totally wrong for another. Only the internal wisdom has the intelligence, sensitivity, and flexibility to determine at any given point what is appropriate for an individual.

Part of what is appropriate involves taking into account our inertia, our tendency to hang on to old ways and habits even when they are no longer suitable. A reactionary element dwells in each of us. The ego feeds on continuity, and feels it necessary for self-preservation. Therefore be gentle with yourself when you experience the inevitable resistance to change. Allow that these processes may take some time. One who is externally oriented doesn't learn in a week or a month the full art of inner listening. Patience and playing lightly with your lifestyle can often bring more change in the long run than the full-steam-ahead approach, although for some people the latter may be just the right thing. Allow time for the different aspects of yourself to adapt to the changes you will be experiencing.

However long it may take, the process of shifting from externally oriented to more internally oriented can begin in a variety of ways. The initiation may be as simple as taking a class in relaxation, beginning to do Yoga, beginning to do your hypnotic process on a daily basis, or inquiring into the cause(s) of all the little headaches and stomachaches that come your way. Once activities such as these are begun, they have their own momentum, and new insights will propel you forward.

We are now ready for the second half of our process, which emphasizes the active role we are to play:

THE INNER WISDOM PROCESS—ACTIVE CHOOSING. In the hypnotic state, give yourself the following suggestion: "I am already experiencing messages from the inner wisdom, and hearing them more and more clearly. Now I am going to have the energy, strength, and intelligence to act on these messages. I will find myself gradually less and less interested in those activities which the wisdom has shown me are detrimental to my health (these activities may be named). When I do anything which gives positive feedback, which makes me feel more healthy or whole, I will find myself naturally gravitating towards such activities, and make them a bigger part of my life. I will be at all times open to new activities which may enter my life, which aid in my growth. I will be happy to act more and more on the messages from my inner wisdom; and as I observe myself becoming more healthy this whole process will be reinforced. I will look upon illness, pain, low energy, negativity, and depression, not as bad states to be fought and overcome, but rather as valuable teachers, essential pieces of information in my learning process, as important to me in their own way as feeling good. I will gladly accept all of these life messages."

It pays to be aware of the lack of support in our society for health-giving pursuits. For example, television commercials repeat endlessly the message that the pain of headache, stomachache, hangover, arthritis, hemorrhoids, and a host of other ailments, is best dealt with by taking a pill to ease the symptom temporarily. Seldom does anyone on TV suggest that you find out how to permanently decrease experiencing such symptoms. Our society has given hearty approval to taking pills also for anxiety, depression, and fear. Most people who experience these forms of important negative feedback either endure them stoically or cover them over chemically. Since they are an urgent call to begin a reevaluation of our whole life, there is great harm in either enduring or covering over these unpleasant feelings. It is necessary to confront them, experience them, determine their origin, and then act. Often experiencing them fully without resisting them can in itself bring about a change in their quality. We begin to see our joys and sorrows not as external phenomena to be manipulated, but rather as an intelligent communication from the depth of ourselves, from the inner wisdom to the outwardly directed consciousness. We don't expect a life free from pain, discontent, annoyance, or illness. Instead, our inner wisdom will allow us to relate to these and all feelings in such a manner that we don't get caught up in negativity or illness.

The role of self-hypnosis can be significant to this process on several levels. First, we can explore ourselves more often and more deeply than we generally do. Besides the overall suggestion to be generally more attuned to the inner wisdom, we can specifically suggest being directly in touch with how we actually feel about some activity, person, or situation. We can explore our bodies, our attitudes, our feelings, our fears, to find out what is there and how we operate. From this self-knowledge, which is the foundation of all real change, the inner wisdom can flourish in us and direct us to a new and healthier quality of being.

12

Enjoying the Holistic Lifestyle

Are you satisfied with the quality of your daily life? When you wake up in the morning, what is that first flicker of consciousness like? Are you truly interested in the prospect of the coming day?

At the very root of things, your health depends on the quality of your daily life. If there is a real interest in what you do, in your relationships, in the world out there and the world within you, then you are very much alive. The wellness scale we mentioned earlier could also be called the aliveness scale—and nothing brings out this quality of aliveness more than interest. In fact, health, aliveness, and interest are three perspectives on one quality. When you are interested in your life, you are less likely to overeat, to turn yourself off, and to do those things which destroy health. Your resistance to disease is high—you are not anxious to interrupt the good thing you've got going. Therefore interest is the greatest medicine, a prime factor in health.

Are you interested in your work? If the answer is "no," it might pay to explore this area seriously. In more primitive cultures people's work is more or less determined for them from the time they are born—often it is laboring in the fields. That is a given task, and they have to live with it.

Even in our culture, which allows an extraordinary choice of occupation and lifestyle, some people get stuck in an unfortunate rut. They move rapidly from childhood to marriage and responsibility, drifting into being a housewife or finding an immediate job to pay the bills. Years go by, and as they get older it becomes harder to awaken that sudden burst of energy needed to break out of old patterns which may no longer be appropriate. Therefore many people get stuck in a situation that fundamentally doesn't interest them, and adopt a resigned attitude towards their work. This attitude seems at the surface one of acceptance, but underneath there is frustration or bitterness. Since their interest level is low, there isn't the energy to break out; as time goes by there is even less interest and less energy. A vicious circle has been created.

The situation would seem hopeless if it weren't for the fact that any person in any situation at any age can begin to tune into the ideas expressed in this book and move towards greater wellness. With this comes increased energy and self-confidence, which brings a new perspective on everything. With this new energy and changed perspective you can begin to ask yourself whether it is possible to find a life's work that truly interests you, or whether you can create a renewed interest for yourself in what you now do. Many people in our culture make a dramatic change in their middle or even older years. What is required is a commitment to explore continually all possible ways of keeping yourself interested. With such a commitment many have found that the impossible becomes a reality.

Much of what we've been saying about one's work also applies to one's relationships. Lacking a satisfying relationship to someone or something is as destructive to good health as the lack of an essential nutrient. If you are living with someone it takes work, dedication, and open communication for the relationship to stay healthy. Without communication there can be no real relationship, and communication requires a real intention to communicate, unfortunately lacking in many relationships. Doctors and psychologists see every day a parade of people who have unhealthy relationships, and who blame the problems on their partners.

It is beyond the scope of this book to go further into the factors that make healthy relationships possible. The same situation applies here as in being happy with one's work: changes in energy and perspective can open new doors in yourself. The only thing that can possibly change the quality of your relationship is a change in yourself. When you become interested in something you make use of all available help. In the last decade there has been a powerful growth in sophistication regarding the art of relating. Some good books have emerged. There are also many workshops, courses, and growth centers which offer exciting new approaches to relating. Again, what it takes is an interest in exploring and a willingness to change.

We've mentioned *how* you spend your time, and with *whom* you spend your time. *Where* you spend your time also contributes to the quality of your health. To take an extreme example, some men work by day in a noisy factory, go from there to congested traffic, and then hang out in a dark, smoky bar, relieving the tensions of the day. Smog, noise, pollution, lack of space—all these expressions of a disharmonious environment get assimilated and can't help but have a negative effect on one's health.

Environment also means the space you create for yourself where you live. Is it filled with chaos, disorder, and continuous loud noise? This, too, is part of your Total Diet and affects your health. Do you have a quiet, relaxing, comfortable space where you can get away from time to time without being interrupted, to help balance out the more stressful aspects of your life? A harmonious environment can fulfill the same function as good food and good relationships. Since you, as an adult, are responsible for your environment, it pays to give consideration to how it affects your being, whether you are satisfied with it, and if not, what you can do about it. You may find that as you become more healthy the quality of your environment begins to feel more and more like the quality of your food, and affects you just as much.

Aside from these highly important factors of work, relationship and environment, where does the *essence* of the holistic lifestyle dwell? Everywhere you look, into every corner of your life, you will see the need for a dynamic balance. Disharmony and disease can be looked upon as a lack of balance. Feeling ill, depressed, or incomplete are all ways the system is telling you, "See to some imbalance that is occurring." The ancients in many cultures sensed balance to be the key factor in living the good life. The Chinese saw the forces in the universe playing as two forms, Yin and Yang, which danced together and complemented each other when things were flowing harmoniously. The Golden Mean of the Greeks held balance as the ideal, in the avoidance of extremes. The real art, of course, is to be able to sense which factors are out of balance, and what to do about it in your own lifestyle.

As usual, the physical plane, being more tangible, is the easiest to recognize and deal with. In terms of diet there must be the proper balance of proteins, fats, and carbohydrates. Many combinations of nutrients require a delicate balance, such as sodium-potassium. Then there is the balance of input and output. Nutrients and calories are the input; exercise, work, physical and psychological movement are the output. With too much input comes overweight, sluggishness, and greater illness of every sort, as well as a shorter life expectancy. With too much output comes exhaustion, premature aging, nervous breakdown, and low resistance to disease. Since life's demands vary continually, the input and the output are never the same, which is why the balance is dynamic, always adjusting itself, rather than static. Of course, there are an enormous number of systems in the body, whose balance must be maintained for optimal health.

You could spend many lifetimes studying the way balance operates on the psychological plane. One example which affects many people is the balance between the desire for newness, variety, adventure, and fresh experience on the one hand, and the desire for security and freedom from hassle on the other. Too much of the former leads to scattered, often chaotic life, dilettantism, never getting focused enough to reach the heart of anything, whether it be a relationship or a pursuit. Too much of the latter leads to dullness, stagnation, and fear of anything new—a crystallized, deadened lifestyle. A healthy life is a dance between the extremes of newness and tradition.

Another important balance to examine in your own life is that between giving and getting. Health professionals often spend far more of their time giving out energy to others and nurturing them than they do receiving energy and being nurtured. Others take a great deal, seeming to suck up all the energy of those they come in contact with, while giving little. Communication is a circular flow of energy, and some kind of an overall balance is necessary between giving and getting for a healthy life. Some people, such as many women approaching middle age who have reared a family, need to learn new ways of getting, of nurturing themselves. People of the other extreme may discover that if they can find some way to give, they suddenly feel very much more alive. The challenging, and sometimes frustrating, fact about seeking balance is that *there are no formulas*; what worked superbly for your friend may be just what you don't need.

One of the most interesting plays of the opposites involves on the one hand taking things very seriously, trying hard, being concerned about how it will all come out versus a relaxed, hang-loose attitude, a freedom from concern, the feeling that it will all work out anyhow. In a given situation one or the other of these attitudes may be totally appropriate; but it pays to become acquainted with any tendencies towards either extreme in your own life, and to see how lack of balance in this domain creates specific problems. Those who are overbalanced on the side of taking things seriously often get high blood pressure, and all the illness that stems from hypertension. Not being able to relax, they often lack a sense of humor or perspective about the events in their life. Those, on the other hand, whose lack of balance goes in the other direction, tend towards superficiality both in what they do and in how they relate. Their interests are often just surface affairs; they frequently gloss over real problems with a veneer of being philosophical or unbothered when it may well be more appropriate to be bothered. A person who is functioning from high level wellness will move rapidly and easily, as situations dictate, between great seriousness and intensity, and an easy, relaxed, good-humored attitude.

For health to flourish yet another kind of balance is needed, the interplay among healing, maintenance, and growth. Healing is the domain of traditional medicine. Part of the holistic lifestyle involves determining what areas aren't working well, and then doing something to improve the situation. This may involve many of the things we have been discussing, including diet changes, exercise, stress reduction, changes in lifestyle, etc. Those who don't put energy here when needed will have a hard time moving towards greater health. But those who concentrate all their energy in healing will be missing out on the two other limbs of holistic health, maintenance and growth.

Maintenance is the heart of preventive medicine. Those areas which are healthy or have been healed need a lifetime of care in order to remain healthy. Occasionally you meet someone with a car that has several hundred thousand miles on it and runs beautifully. Invariably the owner has put a lot of love into its maintenance. If you were to put similar energy into the maintenance of your own machine as a way of life, you would greatly increase the chances of resembling that car well into old age. After reading this far you probably have a good idea of what is involved in maintenance. It means a considered, thoughtful lifestyle, and not just a periodic checkup.

Growth is the third limb, and it means going beyond

what you now know and experience. Growth is an essential ingredient in aliveness, for those who reach a certain level in living and then stop invariably begin to stagnate, to grow dull. To use a dietary example of the three limbs, healing might be to go on a special diet for a while to get through a toxic period. Maintenance would be to adopt sane eating habits as a way of life. Growth would include experimenting with your diet, tuning in more finely to the feedback your body and mind is giving you, refining and changing, never getting stuck in one particular pattern of eating. Growth also involves experimenting with your Total Diet. For example, if you seldom spend time alone, you might try taking a weekend and going to the country just to be with yourself, question your priorities, and get an overview of your life. Growth involves curiosity, questioning, never becoming too satisfied, always being open to change.

If you can possibly take some time when you have energy and are not distracted, you can have a good close look at the total picture of your life to see which areas need healing, which require maintenance, and what areas are open to growth. Become interested in your life as an ecosystem and study its energy flow. Examine the input, physical and psychological. Observe the way you transform this energy, and notice what the output is like. Your output is not only what you get done, but how you come across, the quality of energy you put out into the world. In examining this flow of energy from what you take in to what you give out, you can begin to zero in on leaks of energy, areas of weakness or wastage in the overall flow. For example, if you drink a lot of alcohol this is a major energy leak in your ecosystem. Not enough exercise is another energy leak. So is living in a tense situation, eating too much sugar, not liking what you do, smoking cigarettes, not having a proper balance of intensity and relaxation. There are a vast number of common energy leaks, and each person has his or her own pattern of major and minor leaks. If you are able to discover and do something about these leaks, perhaps with the aid of self-hypnosis, you will find yourself taking a sizable jump towards greater wellness. It is essential of course to work first on the major leaks. Each time you plug up a major leak your system becomes more sensitive, and you will be in a position to locate other, more subtle leaks.

Here is where self-hypnosis can be an enormously valuable tool. To create a personalized health-evaluation program, an accurate assessment of strengths and weaknesses is essential. You've got to know your leaks. Many people are blinded to their own weaknesses for the simple reason that to see them would mean changing, giving something up, which they are afraid to do. Therefore it requires a clear, unbiased awareness and a great receptivity in order to assess what is needed. This is just the quality that comes about naturally in the self-hypnotic state. Here is a process designed to help you get in touch with the state of your being.

THE TOTAL CHECKUP PROCESS. Put yourself into the hypnotic state. Now imagine what to you is the perfect doctor, healer, or health practitioner, and see this person appearing vividly before you. He or she is there to give you a total checkup on every aspect of your being. You want to hear the truth. Your consummate health practitioner will tell you what needs to be healed, what requires only maintenance, and what areas are ripe for growth. Be open and receptive to whatever you get from this process, and don't argue or discuss the response. Sometimes people are surprised by what they find out about themselves. The more surprised you are, the more valuable the process may have been to you. If there is a lull, you may ask specific questions, to which you may or may not get a response.

A slightly different process may also be of value to you, particularly if you are fuzzy, as many are, about just what it is you want. While some people are overly goal-oriented, many others flounder helplessly because they have never taken the trouble to know themselves well enough to establish just what they want, both short- and long-range.

THE PRIORITY PROCESS. Place yourself into the hypnotic state. Then ask yourself, "What is it that I really want? What is important to me? Is there something missing in my life?" Allow time after each question for the pictures or images to come. "Am I spending my time and energy the way I want to be spending it? What are my priorities, both short- and long-range?" It may help afterwards to write down whatever pictures or words came to you, and to contemplate them seriously, because attitudes are central to your being. They not only help determine the way you experience the present, they also have a powerful effect on the future. It pays to be clear about what you want; and it even pays to be clear that you are not clear.

Perhaps the most important item to be clear about from the beginning is whether you are truly committed to being well. That is not a joke. The superficial response of just about everyone is the desire to be healthy; yet if health should mean having to change certain harmful habits, some people are more interested in keeping their habits than in becoming more healthy.

At every moment we have a choice whether or not to opt for wellness. In fact, there exists in us the "Will to Wellness," which is a more general, milder form of the "Will to Live." If the will were functioning simply in us, unmodified by any opposing force, we would all naturally move towards greater health. This, however, is not the case. Another force operates in us, tending to nullify the effect of the will to wellness. It has been called the "Will to Die." It may also be thought of as the will to avoid disturbance, the will to merge and disappear, the desire for ultimate peace. Those who have a preponderance of this drive lead lives which tend towards self-destruction. They frequently kill themselves, rapidly or slowly. In times of great stress one can sometimes observe firsthand the battle going on between the will towards health and life and the will towards destruction and death.

There is such a thing as a commitment to be well. It can make the difference in the direction you move in getting older, as you get pulled by these two opposing drives. This commitment is the realization that you can choose to go along with the will to wellness any time the opportunity arises, while letting the opposing will to destruction alone, not putting yourself in gear with it. The commitment is also a resolve to make this choice to be well, and to continue making it. Just to know you can choose wellness and have it affect your life is a freeing and comforting thought.

THE CHOOSING WELLNESS PROCESS. Through self-hypnosis you can put this commitment immediately into action. In the hypnotic state give yourself this posthypnotic suggestion:

"I am aware that at every moment I can choose between wellness and illness. This fact will be firmly remembered and remain a part of my consciousness at all times. *I choose to be well*. My choice matters, and will from this moment on have its positive effect on my being. My choice to be well will show itself in the way I eat, exercise, relate to others, and in every aspect of my life. It will come out in my attitude towards whatever happens to me. I am from this moment beginning to feel the beneficial effects of this choice to be well. I see clearly that my health depends largely on my attitudes, and that I can, and do, choose my attitude. I choose to be well."

The implications of this attitude are immense. You will begin to see more and more practical applications in your daily life. One application is that you can now begin to make positive use of your strong areas to work on your weak ones. For example, Fred M. was a very physical person. His job as a ranger kept him physically active, and in his spare time he would run, canoe, and climb mountains, usually alone. In his forties his health began to break down, and someone introduced him to the ideas of holistic health. At a certain point the realization dawned on him that he had developed one aspect of his being very highly, almost to the entire exclusion of the psychological and the spiritual. He used his love of sports and outdoor activities to begin taking classes and workshops to expand his interests. In these activities he met new people, got exposed to interesting new perspectives, formed new relationships, and even began to see how sports, when done from a centered, aware state, could be an inroad to the spiritual.

Malcolm R. was the opposite type, an intellectual who felt at home only in the world of ideas and reason, bored with any exercise beyond lifting his beer. As he grew older and paunchier he began to recognize that it was downhill all the way from then on unless he got interested in his body. Yet he was so entrenched in his habits of neglect that he didn't seem to have sufficient push to change. His interest in psychology led him to self-hypnosis, where he came upon the process tailor-made for people like him:

THE INTELLECTUAL MOTIVATOR. When there is something you would like to begin doing and are having trouble starting, sit down as a prelude to hypnosis, and make a list of all the logical reasons why you should change. Make full use of your intellect, let your logic be impeccable and convincing. Then put yourself in hypnosis, and go over every point in the list slowly and carefully. Tell yourself that you will remember the reasoning and see more and more in your daily life how it applies. You will soon begin to see your purely intellectual force, not enough in itself to change you, taking on an emotional quality which has far greater power, and can motivate you in whatever directions you choose.

Malcolm did in fact find reasons, with the help of hypnosis, which were sufficient to get him interested in doing something about his body. He also found that hypnosis provided an added benefit: it helped him discover which goals were realistic for his particular condition, and helped him set up a flexible timetable for achieving these goals.

Many people have too many goals already, and for them goals in the realm of health would create yet more friction and tension in their lives, more frustration and fear of failure. Others, like Malcolm, find that they need goals in order to function, and can work well if their goals are realistic and flexible. Many people set up harsh and un-realistic expectations for themselves, and are continually down on themselves for not living up to them. They fail to take into account the fact that their organism has been used to doing things its own way for a long time, and needs to be nudged gently in new directions, not harshly shoved.

While under hypnosis, Malcolm got in touch with what his organism felt was possible, given its years of mistreat-ment and poor habits. From this information he was able to set up a timetable which allowed for gradual change in his eating and exercise habits. Today he is a healthy man with a new body. There is an obvious sense of enjoyment of living about him.

Too often this central factor of health is glossed over or neglected entirely. The road to optimal health is to enjoy oneself. People who live to a ripe age almost invariably have things they really enjoy doing, or just a general sense of delight in the changing panorama of life. Exercise books, diet books, and spiritual guidelines—all supposedly repre-senting ways of achieving wholeness and health—tend often to ignore this aspect of living, as if the road to health were somehow a gloomy, solemn affair. It is really easy to begin taking oneself, one's state, one's health very seriously, to lose one's sense of humor, to become caught in a kind of grim fanaticism. If that tendency is present, you can remind yourself in your quiet moments under hypnosis that there is also a light, refreshing, enjoyable quality to living. Empha-size that the heavy and the tragic is balanced by the light and the comic, that life has all kinds of moods, and that an important part of living is to be able to take a step back, relax, and enjoy the richness of the show.

As you begin to taste more and more the fruits of real health there may well come a time when it seems appropri-ate to share some of what you have learned along the way. This is a somewhat delicate point. We've all encountered well-meaning zealots who push their particular salvation on others, invariably turning them off. The more pushy a person is, the more attached to results, the less people will be interested in hearing any truth there might be in his words.

Bearing all this in mind, there is still a way of sharing your own discoveries nonfanatically when the timing is appropriate, simply because you have something worth sharing. There are many ways of doing this. If you run or bicycle alone, try inviting a friend to join you. Invite people to dinner and cook them a meal with tasty, healthful food. If a particular book has had meaning for you, give a copy to someone who may be ripe for it, without any long and unnecessary buildup.

If you want to get more deeply involved you can do volunteer work for health-related institutions, such as hospitals or the Red Cross. If there is a holistic health center near you, become involved. If not, consider what it would be like to have in your area a kind of shopping center or supermarket of holistic services. These may include holistic doctors and dentists, nutritionists, holistic psychologists, other specialists with a holistic perspective, acupuncturists, people who do body work, and a counseling service. It could also include classes on all aspects of health. If you have become sufficiently excited by the changes which have been happening in your life, you may even consider the delight in sharing with others what you have found on a professional basis. Careers in health can be most rewarding because they are a very basic way of exchanging energy with the society which has reared you.

The authors got started professionally in self-hypnosis by giving small workshops in their homes. For those of you who have profited sufficiently from self-hypnosis to feel good about teaching it to others, this represents an organic way of putting your energy back into the world. In giving self-hypnosis workshops you can learn continually about the infinite variety of ways this amazing tool can be applied towards creating a better life.

Addendum:
A Manual For Wholeness

What you have read so far has by and large focused attention on health and health problems in a kind of general, or generic way. But to derive the greatest benefit from hypnosis, and indeed, from any health-promoting technique, it is necessary to focus specifically on *you*.

Sometimes, when you have a defined destination, there may be a clearly marked path leading to it. Health, however, is nothing defined, limited, or fixed; therefore, there is no single way to achieve health. Health is rather a dynamic process, changing, shifting, and growing. *It is the by-product of exploring yourself holistically with interest and care.*

In this special addendum, we'd like to show you in some detail just what you can do to begin exploring yourself. If you actually follow the specific suggestions, you will begin to notice some real changes in the way you feel. Health is not measured by a machine, but by the way it feels to be alive. What follows is a flexible program for being more alive.

THE PHYSICAL DIMENSION

Because it is the most concrete, the physical dimension will serve as a good starting point. Although it is measured

149

easily, it is so often neglected that few adults are in prime physical health. The major reason for that involves the quantity and quality of *input*, which for the body is one's diet of food, water, and air.

Diet is the cornerstone of good health: we are what we eat. If we choose to consume significant amounts of junk food, then we have a junkyard for a body. Your body may hold up against that kind of abuse when it is quite young. When it gets older, however, it becomes a prime candidate for early heart disease, stroke, arthritis, cancer, and diabetes. The quality of our daily fuel is responsible to a large degree for how gracefully we age.

In addition to preventing these chronic diseases, there is perhaps an even more important reason to eat with care: it simply feels a lot better to be alive. When our intake is healthful, we are free of heartburn, indigestion, constipation, excess weight, and sluggishness. We feel energetic, vital, and alive. Once we experience this more enjoyable way of existing, it's hard to go back to the old habits and patterns.

The traditional questions of Who? What? When? Where? How? Why? will help us cover nutrition from this new perspective.

Let's start with *Who*. Who are you? Do you really care about your well-being? Are you truly interested in nurturing and loving your body? If so, then good nutrition will begin to emerge naturally if you just choose to have greater health and happiness for yourself. As we all know, however, eating habits imposed harshly on ourselves are likely to produce friction, reaction, and conflict. Therefore, the kind of nutritional improvement that makes the most sense is a slow, gradual, enjoyable change. *That means eating out of concern and loving choice rather than through the effort of "willpower."*

The *Who* involves you as a unique and special being. Who you are determines your nutritional needs, depending upon your body build and genes. The amount of physical labor and psychological stress in your lifestyle will also affect your needs. So will the climate you've chosen to live in, the time of year, and even the degree of environmental pollution. Therefore, the diet that works so perfectly for your friend or for some authority may not be appropriate for you. Also, your nutritional needs are not constant. They may change as you grow older, or as your lifestyle and interests change. Therefore, experiment with yourself, be your own test lab for what works in your individual case.

What to eat is, of course, the standard question in nutrition. Although we just emphasized individual differences, there remain some excellent guidelines which, when followed, lead rapidly to improved health.

The best advice we can offer is this: *eat a more natural diet.* Until recently, most people on earth ate simply. Their foods were grown nearby in fertile soil. They were whole, fresh, unpreserved and unprocessed. In many places, meat was eaten sparingly or reserved for special occasions. So were confections and pastries. The availability of dairy products was usually limited, too. A natural diet consists largely of fresh vegetables and whole grains, nuts and seeds, beans and sprouts, some fruit, and small amounts of meat and dairy products.

Today, Americans eat "special occasion food" daily in large amounts, which places a great strain on our systems, particularly on the heart and blood vessels. Recent research indicates that many Americans get 40 to 50 percent of their calories from fat, which is far too much. Many of these fats come from meat and dairy products, and tend to be saturated. The intake of saturated fats results in the clogging of the blood vessels, the chief factor in cardiovascular disease and the cause of early death in about half of all Americans. Unsaturated fats, on the other hand, don't produce this constricting sludge, and may even be helpful in keeping the system cleaner. The best source of unsaturated fats is cold-pressed vegetable oils which have not been heated in cooking. Heating makes fats more saturated. A careful person will therefore go lightly on fried foods. She or he will also keep a low intake of cholesterol-laden foods such as eggs, shellfish, and butter.

Natural foods are not refined. Refined means denourished; those who eat whole grains, for instance, in processed food form (however "fortified" they may claim to be) are doing themselves a great disservice. Instead of buying white bread, instant rice, canned vegetables, frozen French fries and other supermarket foods, begin to experiment with eating whole grains of various kinds, and eating fresh, raw foods—salad, for instance—which are higher in vitamins, minerals, and fiber.

Another excellent reason for staying away from processed packaged foods is to avoid chemical additives, preservatives, colors, and stabilizers. These are found in abundance in prepackaged foods, and may well be related to the great rise in cancer and a variety of other illnesses. There is no reason for an intelligent adult to put these questionable substances into his or her system. Tell your grocer what you want. If he can't get it, shop elsewhere. Read labels and ingredients carefully. You'll be amazed.

So, what you don't eat is as important as what you do. Besides saturated fats and chemicals, it would be wise to eat far less caffeine, sugar, and salt. Even protein can be overdone. While a minimal amount of protein is important, too much protein can be unhealthful. The natural diet may include meat, fish, chicken, and dairy products, but the proportions will be very modest. By learning to listen to your body's signals, you can develop a real sense of moderation in eating. Eating more than you need of any nutrient, like protein or vitamins, won't do you any good. Speaking of vitamins, it's probably a good idea to take in a bit more of each than is generally available in average foods.

While the *What* in nutrition is frequently discussed and written about, the *When*, which is of great importance, tends to be neglected.

We are creatures of habit, but we should avoid habitual

eating times because that can dull us to the actual needs of the body. Many people follow the clock rather than their own internal signals when they eat: "It's half past twelve, I'd better eat lunch," or "I'm hungry and it's four o'clock, but I'd better not spoil my appetite for dinner." Relying on *internal* rather than external cues may lead to the healthier practice of eating more frequent but smaller meals. Nibbling food is actually a good practice, particularly if you have hypoglycemia, or low blood sugar. The digestive system is given amounts it can handle comfortably, and you come away from a meal feeling alert and able to function.

In reevaluating the ideas of "meal" and "mealtime," it pays to take a special look at evening eating habits. The daily cycle of hormone and enzyme production suggests that the body is better off eating lightly at night. Unhappily, that is the time when we most often tend to overeat. Heavy nighttime eating has an adverse effect on the quality of sleep, and therefore, indirectly on the quality of the whole following day. Try eating lightly at night for a week, and observe how much finer your mornings feel.

Another time to avoid eating is when you are disturbed, upset, or angry. That often leads to upset angry stomachs, and the food doesn't get well digested.

Where we eat is seldom considered. The *Where*, however, can trigger automatic attitudes which prevent us from enjoying our food and getting in touch with our true needs. Ordinarily, we eat in places where others are eating. The external cue is the same every day. The focus shifts away from our body and the enjoyment of its food. Instead, our energy goes into socializing, or, if we're alone, into reading or watching TV. Losing touch with the actual process of eating, we go on "automatic," we eat too much and we really don't taste and enjoy the food.

To break this habit, we might occasionally try following the advice of the old Zen master who said, "While eating, just eat."

It's enjoyable and healthful to sit quietly and eat a bowl

of food, chewing each mouthful well and savoring the flavor and texture without distraction. People who hate to eat "alone," are simply not "being with" their food.

We've just slipped into the *How*, which greatly affects the quality of our nourishment. How to eat is part of the art of living. Those who arrange their lives so that they're pressed for time when eating are often the ones with the most digestive difficulties. The tension that comes from haste also prevents the body from assimilating the nourishment in the food. The whole popular concept of "fast food" is anti-health.

Nurturing oneself is a prime activity, and should take some precedence in the hierarchy of needs. *Eat slowly, savor each bite, and allow every mouthful to fill you*. Feel each bite as it goes down, follow it and imagine what's happening to it, realizing how this living substance which you're taking into yourself is going to nourish you. You may find that by doing this you get more nourishment with less food.

You might also want to look at the food before you eat it to see if it is something you really *want* to become part of your tissues and bones. To have a moment of focused consciousness just before eating will help you enjoy the meal more, and help your body receive maximum benefit.

Being more conscious of the act of eating will also show you something interesting about the amount eaten. Eat until you are full, and notice a few minutes later how you feel weighed down and sluggish. If, on the other hand, you eat not to fullness but just until you no longer have hunger, and then stop, you'll notice that *a few minutes later* you feel quite satisfied. And whereas before, you might not have been able to function well after eating, you can now function perfectly well. The body's message is loud and clear: *stop eating the moment you lose your hunger*.

The final question is "*Why* do we eat?" Perhaps the most important question of all, *Why* involves our whole psychological attitude towards eating. Few people in our culture eat simply to maintain their life process in optimal fashion. They eat instead for psychological reasons which are sometimes at variance with the physical health of the organism. Perhaps they are not getting sufficient physical or psychological nourishment, or "strokes." Food becomes the substitute.

Another frequent reason for eating is the desire to turn off. Overeating dulls the system; whatever is being felt at the moment loses its intensity and sharpness. A person feeling lonely, upset, or depressed may eat just to turn down the intensity of the negative feeling. When that becomes the pattern, it can lead to overweight, dullness, and losing touch with oneself.

When you see yourself going for that box of cookies and there's no physical hunger, take a moment. Stop and inquire what is going on. Find out what you are really craving, or what you are trying to avoid feeling. That can be an excellent inroad to self-exploration. *Discover the effect you are seeking, and ask yourself whether something other than food might serve as a substitute.* At the very least, look for healthier foods to replace the unwholesome ones which purely psychological cravings so often involve.

What we're talking about here is a long-term change in eating habits designed to be an effortless part of daily living. Going on a typical "diet" is a mere reaction, not a long-term change. If you eat badly and too much, you might typically react by starving yourself, in hopes of returning to normal. But diets almost never work. When they are over, so much stress has accumulated in the effort to maintain them that you tend to explode into old patterns with vengeance. Only a way of eating which involves the effortless enjoyment of good food has any long-term value.

Food is taken into the body so that the nutrients and chemicals can be circulated to every cell, helping to replenish and nourish them. Air and water by this definition may equally be considered food. The oxygen in air is vital to life. Impure air holds many other chemicals besides oxygen, some of which interfere with important body processes. A feeling of going to the mountains or seashore and breathing really clean air is so positive because you are actually getting vitally nourished. The person interested in holistic health will consider the quality of the air and water he or she takes in on a daily basis. They are an important part of your diet.

To get full benefit from input, or food, it has to be properly assimilated and digested. These processes are part of the *inner dynamics* of the body. Here the input gets transformed so that it may do useful work (output). The proper assimilation of food occurs when, in a relaxed state, we eat slowly, chewing thoroughly. For using oxygen, a good set of lungs, properly used, is indispensable. Bad posture and the habit of shallow breathing help to keep the lungs from the full, deep breathing activity they were designed to perform. This detracts from good health.

You can do two things, starting right away, to begin feeling healthier. The first is to perform five or ten minutes a day of a good deep breathing exercise. If you do Hatha Yoga, breathing (called pranayama) is a part of it. If you don't know how to begin, try sitting with your back erect and breathing in and out slowly, deeply, and regularly. Fill and empty the lungs to capacity. Do it only as long as it feels good; if it's at all painful or unpleasant, stop. Anybody of any age can do this, and it will always improve the health.

The second way of using your breathing is to be aware from time to time of your breath during the day, particularly if you are a bit upset. If you become aware of your breath right now as you're reading this, you will see how merely becoming conscious of breathing changes it. When you are upset your breathing becomes shallow and irregular. The emotions affect breathing; it works the other way, too. Good breathing in times of stress helps return the system more quickly to a state of healthy equilibrium.

Digestion is also an important part of the inner physical dynamics. Indigestion, gas, heartburn, or sometimes a foul mood can all result from inefficient digestion. With proper input and a system free from too much stress, the digestion (and all the other countless processes of the body) can proceed without needing to send signals, usually painful, which indicate something isn't working right. When things function smoothly in our bodies we don't notice them; such are the inner dynamics of a healthy person.

We've mentioned that one of the necessary health factors is freedom from too much stress. On the physical plane, stress can be alleviated by getting some kind of massage or similar body work at least once a week. We live with a great deal of stored tightness in the body. Unfortunately we get used to carrying it around, and it loses its effectiveness as a signal for us to do something about the imbalance in our nervous system.

Part of our inner dynamics consists of a proper balance between our two nervous systems. One of them comes into play when we feel we are threatened. It tightens muscles and prepares us for combat or rapid retreat. The other is designed to operate after the reason for the tension is gone or dealt with. This second nervous system relaxes all the muscles in the body, so that energy can circulate freely, helping to heal and repair whatever needs help. What this means is that physical relaxation is essential for a balanced nervous system, and for real healing to occur. Few things accomplish this end as well as physical touch or nurturing.

In our culture we tend to overlook the importance of touch. Current thinking says that the human animal needs to be touched and stroked throughout its life, from the time of birth right through old age. What is this need to be touched? Is it a need to feel loved, or to feel tangibly connected with something outside oneself? Does touching allow some relief from the feeling of separateness? Whatever the reasons, touching seems to reach all dimensions of a person. We recommend more touching in daily life. Look upon massage not merely as a sensuous luxury for an occasional indulgence, but rather as a highly beneficial investment in optimal health.

The quality of the input and the efficiency of our inner

dynamics will help determine the output. In one sense, what we do, how we move in the world, is our physical output. From the holistic standpoint, exercise is the most important physical output. Although your own personal exercise will be unique in what you do and how you do it, we can indicate broadly what kinds of exercise are most conducive to overall health. They fall into two basic categories: those that focus on stretching the body, and the more vigorous ones that get the system really going over a period of time.

Few activities contribute more positively to health than activities which slowly stretch the muscles. These include some dances, Tai Chi, stretching exercises, and especially Yoga. These keep the system flexible, and therefore far more youthful and full of life. They are ideal for relaxing tension. To start the day with such exercise brings a calm, centered quality which lasts into the day. To exercise in this way for a few minutes after completing the work of a tension-filled day changes the quality of the entire evening. The stress gets released in a marvelously efficient recycling process.

Such activity is highly beneficial to the muscles and joints. The stiffening which accompanies aging gets slowed down or even reversed. The arteries remain flexible and arthritis is kept away. Since Yoga is a particularly excellent holistic exercise, we will describe how you can get started immediately, to see if it interests you. If your interests lie in other directions, it is important to follow them. To enjoy doing a physical activity is a most powerful reason for choosing that activity.

Yoga is best learned directly through a good teacher. If your phone book has no Yoga listing, the next best thing is a good book. However you begin, bear this in mind: approach each posture slowly and carefully. Avoid stretching beyond your capacity. Your body lets you know its limits very clearly; listen to its message. What often prevents hearing the body's message is having an image of a completed posture from watching someone else or seeing a picture, and then trying to duplicate the position even if your body isn't ready for that amount of stretch. This leads to injury and frustration.

Instead, try stretching slowly to a point just at the edge of comfort. The muscles are challenged, but not strained. It should feel more or less intense, and definitely *not* painful. If there's pain, you have stretched too far. *Be interested in the way it feels, rather than in how far you are stretching.* Loosening will come by itself as time goes on.

There are many different types of stretches. Most people should probably do some spinal flexibility exercises. These include forward bends, back bends, and spinal twists. The topsy-turvy poses like the headstand and shoulderstand are good for the entire body, and they especially stimulate the glandular system. No matter what your age or degree of stiffness, there are postures that you can begin working on to your advantage.

For losing weight Yoga can be a big help. The postures themselves tend to slim certain areas like the hips and thighs, and generally make the body more compact and trim. In addition, Yoga creates a more sensitive body. That makes it harder to overindulge, and weight loss naturally follows without effort. Finally, being more in touch with your body, you can better tell what foods to eat and, most important, when to stop. This helps prevent the system from getting clogged with food, which is a major contributing factor to illness.

It is no wonder, then, that Yoga has existed for thousands of years. It is a complete holistic system of exercise. Besides limbering up the body, it emphasizes self-exploration and relaxation, making it a perfect physical tool for total health. If you can spare twenty minutes once or twice a day for Yoga, it will be time well spent.

In addition to the slow, stretching kind of exercise, there remains the more traditional kind of dynamic exercise, equally important for good health. Running, swimming, bicycling, and many competitive sports fall into this category, where there's actually a high increase in the heat and energy output. The kind we particularly recommend is exercise involving rhythmic repetition. This is unlike tennis, where you may be running, then standing still, then stretching hard for a long shot. We suggest something more like gentle jogging or a rapid walk where the movement of the body is rhythmic, repetitive, and perhaps bouncy. This gets the heart rate going, the blood circulating, the breath moving, the lungs expanded, and the whole system operating at a level of fuller throttle for perhaps ten or fifteen minutes. If you increase the time gradually you will feel still healthier. You will probably need less sleep and digest your food better. Your heart will be able to work less hard and your arteries will become cleaner passages for blood to flow unimpeded. Thus you will offer yourself a distinct measure of protection against heart disease and stroke.

For complete health you should do both the stretching and the vigorous exercise. Whatever exercises you do, try to get off to a good start by doing them very regularly. The more you begin to skip days, the harder it is to get back into any exercise. Begin modestly, find an activity you enjoy doing for its own sake, and do it at a level you can live with comfortably.

THE PSYCHOLOGICAL DIMENSION

How do you assess the state of your psychological health? Is there the equivalent of healthy input and proper exercise? What is a smoothly functioning inner dynamic, analogous to good digestion? What can you actually *do* to improve your health psychologically?

Part of the psychological input can be organized situations which provide food for growth. Gestalt groups of all sorts offer various kinds of focus for awareness, sensitivity, and relationship. It is difficult to be in such a group and not have more of oneself come to the surface. That can be freeing and health-giving. *It takes energy to hold part of ourselves under lock and key, as most of us do.* For some people, groups can be tremendously helpful because of the confidential, trusting environment which they create. In such an environment, one can begin to allow hidden parts of oneself out into the open, encouraged and supported by feedback from others.

Often, attitudes of unresolved conflict stemming from the earliest memories of one's parents are expressing themselves in all of one's present relationships. This unresolved quality may come out in various ways. An overblown need for approval, the need to be the center of attention, an inability to express warmth and positivity, a sexual tightness, or fear of intimacy may all have to do with accumulated mental debris which has not yet been processed. Groups of all sorts can take you far towards processing some of this debris, freeing your system from psychological toxins and allowing you to taste a new kind of health.

Another alternative is a private relationship with a therapist, counselor, or some other professional listener. For some people, particularly those in an intensive growth phase, which is often painful, there is more opportunity in working with an individual because they have a whole hour to themselves. In a group you can't take an undue proportion of time without arousing bad feelings. One-to-one relationships can have a depth which may be important during times of intensive transformation or change. Also, many people are simply not desirous of or ready to risk sharing the subtle, scary contents of their minds with a group of almost-strangers. One disadvantage of a therapist is the usually high cost. Both individual and group experiences have their assets and their drawbacks.

Traditional psychoanalytic therapists and psychiatrists generally focus on past experiences, often very early ones, to free you ultimately in the present. Behavioral therapy emphasizes more your outer behavior and its consequences in your environment. The more modern, humanistic ap-

proaches, such as Gestalt and psychosynthesis, center on
your experience of the present as an inroad to breaking
through problems. The emphasis is on self-knowledge
through deepening your consciousness in the present moment. If you are interested in expanding your input psychologically, there are good books, classes, seminars, and
groups through which you can find out more in any field that
whets your appetite.

Why would a person, obviously sane and well-
functioning, consider going to outside sources like groups
and therapists? One excellent reason for getting outside
help is the presence of a common dis-ease of the psyche:
feeling poorly about oneself. Just as daily stomach cramps,
being a form of feedback, would cause pretty fast response
of some sort, so not liking oneself is also a form of feedback
which cries out for remedial attention. It means the machine
is using up a large percentage of its vital energy in unnecessary internal friction.

Other people respond unfavorably to someone sending
out the message of self-dislike. These negative responses
cause the person to dislike him/herself even more, which
affects his/her behavior adversely, and so on in a vicious
circle. Also, the more people dislike themselves, the more
fault they find with others, and the less satisfying any
relationship feels. Those people who are highly critical of
others are highly critical of themselves. It is difficult for
such people to get the nurturing they need. Even good
input, such as a compliment, is neither accepted nor believed. *The tightness involved in relating from an inner
posture of self-dislike is a major contributor to ill health.*

If you see the importance of liking yourself, it would
pay at this point to do a little emotional assessment. Here
are some questions to ask yourself. Answer them as much as
possible without employing your analyzing, judging, rational faculty. Just ask and let the answer pop into a
receptive mind.

"Do I like myself? Do I judge myself much? Negatively

or positively? When I think about myself, what do the thoughts feel like? Are there many self-critical thoughts? Do I divide myself up into a horse and rider, with the rider frequently whipping the horse, and sometimes holding a carrot just beyond reach? If there are many self-critical thoughts, what are they about? What don't I like about myself? (A remarkably accurate clue for answering this one is found in what you don't like in others—usually you are resisting that same trait in yourself). Am I defensively supportive of myself? Do I feel a strong need to be right? Do I have high standards which I often seem incapable of living up to? Do I put much energy into making others wrong?"

"Yes" to the last four questions also indicates a strong feeling of doubt about your worth. Now, finally, after having paused and remained with each question, ask yourself, "How do I feel about myself?"

The inner dynamics of the psyche depend on a certain amount of smooth, friction-free movement. Self-dislike is like sand in the wheels. If through examination you determine that you don't like yourself too well, groups or therapy can play a major role in returning you to the naturally healthy state of liking yourself. (This is not to be confused with a person who has an inflated opinion of himself, which is really a cover-up for doubts about his own worth.)

It is also important not to depend entirely on others for your well-being. Just as exercise is work *you* do to participate in becoming more healthy, there is also psychological work to be done. The fundamental purpose of therapy and group work is to make you healthier by allowing what is now unconscious to become conscious. The light of consciousness is the only thorough way of dissolving self-destructive behavior.

Your psychological participation in the process of becoming truly healthy is just as important as your physical participation, although it is harder to define. Your object is to see yourself the way you actually *are*, not the way you *should* be or would *like* to be. This involves suspending judgment. When you judge, you can't see anything clearly. Whatever you see, allow it fully and consciously to be. This simple act of suddenly becoming conscious of the way things are inside you and outside you, and then allowing them all to be, is a practical kind of inner work that you can begin doing right now, which will have as important an effect on your life as any exercise. It will enable you to see and then drop all those little resistances which are the source of all unnecessary stress.

One of the major lessons to be learned from doing this exercise is the realization that nobody else is responsible for our emotional life. We begin to experience the truth that however we are feeling at this moment is a creation of our own mind. To see this fully implies that we stop blaming others for our situation. Taking the responsibility, as adults, for our own state, means that we are no longer putting up the barrier of blame. It means that we can begin to listen openly to others just as we learn to listen to ourselves without judgment.

Creative listening is a real art. In close relationships there is normally a tendency to hear what we want to hear. Whatever is not in our self-interest to hear we distort, repress, or ignore. Total listening involves not only understanding words; the majority of what is communicated is at a nonverbal level. The look in the eyes, the posture, the tone of voice, the things left unsaid, and all the subtle gestures contribute to a rich, multidimensional message which is being sent all the time underneath verbal communication. A sensitive listener picks up on the total message, including contradictions between the verbal and the nonverbal. An enormously high amount of stress in our lives comes directly from the breakdown of communication in relationships. If this is a troublesome area for you, a simple exercise might help you pinpoint just where difficulties in communication lie.

When there is a disagreement or an argument brewing, the two parties each agree to repeat the gist of what the other has said immediately afterwards, to the other's complete satisfaction. For example, if your mate says something critical of you, the normal response is to get your hackles up, a defensive posture which makes it hard to hear the message. Instead, using this exercise, you are placed in a position where you must listen well enough to be able to repeat the criticism. If your mate is satisfied that you have heard and understood, then you get to give your response, and your mate has to satisfy you that it has been understood. While not leading to the most flowing, spontaneous conversation, this exercise nevertheless opens up entirely new possibilities in communication. Disagreements have a very different flavor when you feel you are being heard.

As in the physical plane, the output on the psychological plane will depend on the quality of input and the working of the inner dynamics. Groups, therapy, books on psychology, seminars, classes, can all serve as valuable new input. Combined with an inner dynamic which processes the input fully, allowing your whole being to tell its story uninterrupted by judgment, this will yield a new quality of psychological output. Improved relationships, deeper communication, negative states which are more transient, and an overall feeling of psychological well-being underneath your various moods are all aspects of the psychological output which may be expected as you move towards greater wellness.

THE SPIRITUAL DIMENSION

Normally in our culture we tend to make a clear-cut distinction between the religious or spiritual aspects of life, and the rest of it. The holistic life makes no such distinctions. We are at all moments in relationship, and this relationship extends outwards ultimately to include the rest of the universe. The spiritual includes a deep sense of this relationship, which profoundly affects all areas of daily life.

To feel connectedness and to be spiritually in touch are two ways of indicating the same thing. Therefore what on the physical plane is illness, on the psychological plane depression or anxiety, is on the spiritual plane alienation: the feeling of being cut off, separate, uninvolved, isolated. This is often accompanied by a sense of meaninglessness.

A prime human need, perhaps as great as the need for good food, exercise, and relationships, is the need to feel a part of something more than oneself. People tolerate great injustice and undergo much hardship in order to be part of something, to belong to a greater entity. Joining an organization, a political party, a particular religion, comes from the desire to be part of something greater. The spiritual feeling involves being part of something greater without excluding a particular part of the universe. Exclusion by an individual or by an organization leads to that feeling of alienation which is the indication that one is living in a tiny space, a very small part of the total consciousness possible to the individual. We call this little space the ego, the separate individual aspect of oneself. There is nothing "wrong" with the ego and nothing "wrong" with the feeling of alienation. There *is* a need felt in the depths of one's being to fulfill, to complete, to go beyond, to evolve. Experiencing alienation is an incentive to explore the spiritual dimension of living.

Imagine someone born and raised in a small, dark cell, and conditioned from earliest childhood to believe that this cubicle was it. He is content to live there, knowing nothing else. He amuses himself the best he can by walking around, decorating the cell, and lying down on the cot, dreaming. Everything goes along smoothly, with the usual little ups and downs. Then one day he begins to feel a little empty, as if there were perhaps something missing which is very important. He invents theories and speculates in order to keep comfortable with what he's got, but a growing sense of discontent begins to be felt in his life. From somewhere deep down, he senses the existence of pastures, mountains, oceans, and blue sky. This feeling, perhaps vague at first, is the initial and most important step in ultimately being out of the prison.

The prison is our ego, our limited viewpoint. Its existence always results in defending this little space against outside threat. There is much fear, tightness, and violence connected with this whole process, and here lies one of the major connections between the spiritual (wholeness) and holistic health.

No organism can be truly healthy if it is using up a large amount of its energy in defending itself against what is felt to be a hostile universe. A healthy animal is aware of immediate danger, but doesn't feel the universe as a continual threat. So the experience of being cut off can act as a trigger to do something in the same way that a chronic pain or depression moves us.

However, you don't need to feel cut off to explore the spiritual realm. Many people have had experiences, variously labeled as enlightenment, oneness, cosmic consciousness, peak experience, total love, or any of the many names for those deeply felt religious feelings that come when they realize they are not separate. These feelings are sometimes triggered by drugs, fasting, extreme exertion, or sensory deprivation. Often they occur in the midst of ordinary life, an unexpected moment of grace which can leave a mark for a lifetime, perhaps instigating a spiritual quest. Many who improve their health holistically, who eat better, exercise more, learn to relax and to feel better about themselves, have reported an increase in the number of such spiritual experiences. Growth in one realm tends to breed growth in other realms.

Aside from spontaneous realizations, there are traditional paths to the spiritual life. In our culture, as in many, service and prayer are two of the most common ways. From our perspective of holistic health, we can understand them both in a special fashion. Service is the spontaneous enjoyable action which flows from the understanding that my deepest interest and well-being is furthered when I expend

some of my energy on others in a helpful way. The more I
see how things work, the more apparent it is that the world's
interest and mine coincide. So service is not a duty one does
in order to become more spiritual. Rather, it is a way of
relating to others that makes one feel good, that seems to
have a healing, opening effect on one's being.

Prayer can mean many things. For us it means not so
much asking the Deity to change the universe on our behalf.
It is instead a state in which the mind has ceased its frantic,
self-centered pursuit, and is in communion with what is
taking place. It is a state of total inclusion which expresses
wholeness and promotes health. A more suitable word
might be "meditation." This quality of meditation is an
important doorway to finding out about yourself in a deep,
direct way.

Despite what has been associated with the word, there
is nothing mysterious or supernatural about meditation. You
can begin doing it without necessarily embracing a teacher,
formal instruction, or a particular viewpoint. In fact, meditation takes you beyond all particular viewpoints. You don't
have to be able to sit cross-legged for long periods. If you
would like to try meditating, sit comfortably in any fashion,
preferably with your back erect. The reason for this is that
your posture is directly related to your mental quality: a
physical slouch tends to encourage a psychological slouch.
Equally, a tense, rigid back creates a tense, rigid mind. An
erect, relaxed spine encourages an alert mind which is also
calm, the perfect quality for meditating.

Once you've established yourself physically, what do
you do? The answer is simple: you don't "do" anything in
the normal sense. You merely watch what is taking place,
particularly inwardly. You will notice a succession of
thoughts parading by, thoughts about the past and future,
about money, sex, food, relationships, problems, and every
aspect of your life. Let them all be and watch them.
Observe how when you begin to think about a certain
topic you get lost in it, it takes you over, hypnotizes

you, and removes you from experiencing the present moment.

It is strange how when thought is going on, it is very difficult to be experiencing the present moment. When you see or hear something beautiful, at that moment you are not thinking about dinner; otherwise you are no longer experiencing the beauty. If you suddenly stop thinking about dinner, the mind is quiet, and in that quietness lies the sensitivity to experience fully what is taking place. When your mind is quiet there is no more the endless pursuit of the ego, with its demands for pleasure, power, control, and security. Meditation is an exploration in quietness, a direct experience of the Now from moment to moment without the interference of thought. There is nothing you need to do except watch what is taking place.

"But," you may ask, "I've tried it, and my mind seems perpetually filled with thought. How do I stop thinking?"

You'll find that if you resist thought, that this is merely thought doing battle against thought, which breeds tension. However, if you follow thought for a while, it begins to slow down by itself, and there are spaces between thoughts. Some people like to focus on their breathing to help the mind be quiet. Others focus on a particular word, which is called a "mantra," which also helps the mind cease its chatter. Any word will do, although some words seem to have a particular resonance.

Whether you focus on something or just observe the flow of events, the main thing to remember is that no effort is required. Everything taking place is equally all right. There is no need to judge anything or to resist. It is a great relief when you finally realize that nothing is "supposed" to happen, that there are no "shoulds" in meditation.

That meditative quality, that awareness of what is taking place without judgment, can be with you at any time during the day, and not only when you are sitting quietly. You suddenly become aware of your existence underneath the train of thought, and for a moment you are dehypnotized. That is the inner dynamic of the spiritual realm, and will enrich your life greatly if you do it.

Just as people have different tastes in music, so do they have different tastes in spirituality. Your own personal spiritual input will depend on your taste. Some thrive with the religion they were brought up on. Others find it necessary to dismiss their religion, either coming back to it later from new perspectives, or striking out in other directions. To many, the spiritual input includes seminars, workshops, gatherings, camps, retreats, and any coming together of like-minded individuals for the purpose of finding out more about themselves and the universe. Some will find a single religion or teacher, others will learn from various sources as they move through life. The sources of your spiritual input may expand as you grow, so that anything, anybody, even life itself can be your teacher.

Your output spiritually can't be measured in terms of any particular activity. Rather, it is a quality of being which reflects to what extent your self-protective, egotistical way of functioning has evaporated in the light of knowing yourself. Spiritual output, simply stated, is compassion for others.

CREATING YOUR OWN UNIQUE PROGRAM

What is the best way of putting what has been learned so far into practice in daily living? Since people's individual health needs are as unique as fingerprints, your total well-being is best served by devising a program tailor-made to suit your own needs. Here is a step-by-step guideline for creating your own personal pathway to greater holistic health.

First, to create a suitable program, you have to be accurately in touch with the present state of your health. A mini-checklist of key areas will give you a broad view of your situation, and help indicate to you which directions to take. Take time to answer the following three questions.

Write down your answers. This helps by encouraging you to search yourself more deeply. Also, writing often reveals factors which had been hidden, and helps organize your thinking. So with each question write whatever pops into your mind, without a great deal of self-analysis. Since by now it is apparent that health displays itself on the psychological and spiritual planes as well as on the physical, make sure to answer each question in terms of all three categories. It helps to find a quiet place in order to just be with these questions, seeing if you can feel the answers as well as think them.

The first question: "How healthy am I now?"

The second question: "What are my major health hazards and health potentials?" Hopefully, having read this far you will have a feeling for which are your strong and weak areas in the physical, psychological, and spiritual realms. You will be able to answer more fully and accurately if you remember not to judge yourself for whatever weaknesses you discover. Instead, be interested in the third question: "What am I doing about my situation?" Before reading on, why not actually take the time now to write down your own answers to these questions?

Okay, with these answers in mind, consider which areas in your life need something new to happen. At this point the second step is to formulate goals and priorities for yourself. These can be long-range and short-range. Let's say you discovered a real lack in your physical health stemming from insufficient exercise. You make a goal to develop your health through proper exercise, gradually and sanely. Your immediate goal is to get started right away on some suitable program and follow it faithfully. Or perhaps you have a problem area in your relationship with your mate. Then you might place a much higher priority on spending more time together, sharing and enjoying as well as working things out.

Be realistic with your goals. If you set them too high you will experience frustration. If you are rigidly attached to your goals you will lack the flexibility necessary to meet changing situations gracefully. Also, too much reliance on achievement of goals takes you away from the importance of the present moment. Let them be flexible guidelines for your behavior; take them seriously without letting them take you over.

Third, after formulating your goals it is important to establish an attitude that leads towards health. That means a commitment to be well. Part of the will to live is the will to be well. In many of us, this will is buried under habit and the continual demand for immediate gratification. For instance, if you are smoking cigarettes, the force of your habit and the desire for that hit of nicotine has clouded over the natural impulse towards health. At any moment you can choose health. If you really want to be well you can make the commitment to choose whatever promotes wellness. If your commitment is serious you will find that the force of habit and the desire for gratification begin to lose their hold over you.

That doesn't mean your life is transformed in an instant. It does mean that you no longer sit back passively and just allow negative factors to go on unheeded. You choose to take an active interest in them, in exploring every possible avenue that leads to the positive. It means you begin to make little experiments, cutting down alcohol or drugs, meditating a little every day, running, or joining a group. Whatever grows naturally out of choice and interest will be more likely to stay with you than something you impose harshly on yourself.

Fourth, you can help bring the physical, psychological, and spiritual into balance by doing more things which nurture and develop all three simultaneously. Yoga is one such activity. It provides the highest quality physical conditioning on one level, a deep psychological relaxation on another, and on a third level the means for getting more in touch with the universe through getting in touch with oneself. Anything we do which helps on all three levels is like a jewel in our lives. Gardening, too, can fit this category.

It provides good physical exercise plus nourishing home-grown food, a sense of quiet relaxation, and a feeling of participation in an ancient cycle, taking from the earth and giving back. Going for a walk in a quiet place with a friend can provide physical invigoration, warm, nourishing companionship, and the spiritual food found in communing with the harmony that is nature. You might consider such activities as being vital to a good, balanced holistic diet.

Fifth, you can use your strengths to work on your areas of weakness. If, for example, you feel strong in the physical department and shy with human relationships you might sign up for a hike with an outing club, or join a jogging class. This would nudge you towards relating more, but in a context that was somewhat familiar and comfortable. If, on the other, you felt more need of exercise, you might find a friend in the same situation and agree to swim, bike, run, or do Yoga together. If you, enjoy relationship but haven't explored much in the spiritual realm, you might help bring more balance in your life by joining a class, workshop, or retreat involved with the spiritual.

Just as your body needs exercise to avoid premature degeneration, so does your mind need frequent new stimuli. Staying interested in living is a necessary component of health; one way of doing this is to involve yourself in newness in a regular way. Read about new things. Take a fresh route home or travel to some new place. Say hello at work to someone you have never related with. Try a new kind of cooking. The less-traveled path is energizing; it keeps you flexible, youthful and above all, interested as you get older. Therefore the sixth step in your program is to do something new each day.

To sum up, here are the six steps for creating your own unique program towards real health:

1. Write the answers to our three questions to determine strengths and weaknesses.
2. Formulate your goals and priorities.

3. Make the choice and commitment to be well.

4. Do more things involving all three aspects simultaneously—physical, psychological, and spiritual.

5. Use areas of strength to work on areas of need.

6. Do something new each day.

WHAT IF YOU DO GET SICK?

No matter how careful you are, it is likely that you will experience from time to time some form of symptom or illness. From the holistic perspective, this is not a "bad" thing, it isn't something which "shouldn't" happen. Rather, think of illness as a valuable message, as a form of feedback from yourself to yourself about something connected with your immediate life. If, for example, a person begins wearing herself out through too much uninterrupted activity, the first message, gentle and quiet, may be a simple feeling of exhaustion. That is a directive to relax and do nothing strenuous until reservoirs of energy get filled again. Often such messages are ignored. An extra cup of coffee, a pill, another engagement, and one carries on with the hectic business of living. Therefore, another message is required, one which is more of a jolt to the system. It is as if the system is saying, "Look, when I send a gentle message you don't pay any attention, or you offer some excuse rather than heeding the message. So I now have to come on stronger in order to protect myself."

The next level of message might be a bad cold, tiredness, an aching feeling all over which makes a few days in bed seem mighty attractive. From a holistic standpoint, this sickness is a blessing, for it strongly encourages the person to do what is most appropriate for her health—to spend a few days relaxing and recharging. Looking upon illness in this way, she doesn't fight or resist it. That has two advantages: first, the experience of the illness needn't be an unpleasant one; second, the illness will heal a lot faster when it isn't being resisted.

So a sickness is a message, and interpreting that message is up to you. It may be saying that you have to watch more carefully what you take into your system. Or it may be an indication of stress which has not been dealt with adequately. Negativity in relationship which has not been worked through can store itself in the system, accumulating literally as a toxin, with the same effect as physical toxins.

Begin to observe the fluctuations in your health, the ups and downs of how you feel, and see if you can correlate this with the events in your life and with how well you are treating yourself. You will soon get the idea that your fluctuations are not random, but are the result of what *you* are doing, how *you* are responding to the challenges of life. Your messages, whether they are physical (sickness), psychological (depression, anxiety), or spiritual (alienation, meaninglessness) are telling you that *you* are responsible ultimately for your state.

At bottom this is a very hopeful message, for it means a deep shift in attitude from dependence on external remedies to dependence on your own capacity to heal yourself.

We have been deeply conditioned to respond whenever we get a symptom with an automatic attempt to get rid of it as rapidly as we can. Aches are seen as a nuisance to be drowned out by chemicals. So the content of the message gets shoved under the carpet, and one no longer thinks about why the symptom is there and what it is trying to say. Total reliance on pills, potions, medicines, or herbal cures merely perpetuates the problem by suppressing the symptom. It's not that one should never take anything for pain. The important factor is to give great significance to the nature of the message, to what lies behind the pain, and to do something about that as well as about the pain.

Seen in this light, doctors play a very different role. A holistic life makes use of available information, and a good holistic doctor can be an excellent advisor or counselor. To make use in this fashion of a doctor as one more resource in your own health program is to take the responsibility for

your own health. For many, however, the doctor is the
ultimate external remedy. Instead of going to the store to
buy a chemical for getting rid of a symptom, they go to a
doctor who tells them what chemical to buy. Looking in this
way at the doctor as one who is supposed to heal them, they
abandon their own responsibility, they give up their own
vital role in their own healing process. A doctor is a person
who can help and guide us. Ultimately, however, you
become your own best physician, therapist, and guru.

The more you explore yourself in the light of what is
contained in this book, the more of a feeling you will get for
how to respond should illness come your way. There is great
beauty and freedom in being your own doctor-therapist-
master. By accepting who you are and what you are, you can
move more and more towards total well-being.

Index

A

Accident-prone people, 95
Additives, chemical, in food, 152
Adrenaline flow, control of, by hypnosis, 63-64
Advertising, suggestion used in, 12-13, 135
Aerobic exercise. *See* Exercise
Alpha state, of consciousness, 3-4
American Indians, use of hypnosis by, 19-20
Anger, after hypnosis, 50
Animal Magnetism theory of hypnosis, 20
Anxiety, relief by hypnosis, 64
Aura, caused by body's energy, 101
Automobiles, doing self-hypnosis in, 30-31
Autosuggestion. *See* Self-hypnosis

B

Balance, on physical plane, 139, 141-42
on psychological plane, 140, 143-48
Balancing system, of body, self-hypnosis' effect on, 31
Bedtime, self-hypnosis at, 30, 51
Being part of it all process, for high level wellness, 123-24
Blood pressure. *See* Hypertension
Breathing, as deepening method, 36-37
for relaxation, 69
for wellness, 156

C

Caffeine, 152
stress reduction and, 65

Car trip deepening method, 38

Cassettes, use in self-hypnosis, 39

Chaining, of hypnosis methods, 43

Chanting, as induction method, 34

Choosing wellness process, for self-awareness, 145-46

Collective Unconscious, of Carl Jung, 4

Commercials, television. *See* Television commercials

Communication, in relationship, 137-38

Communion with food process, for habit modification, 85-86

Concentration, as ingredient of self-hypnosis, 7-8

Conditioning, against belief in inner wisdom, 131-32

in daily lives, 12-13

Convergence induction method, 33

Coping mechanisms, for trauma, 59-60

D

Daydreaming, 12

Deepening methods, for self-hypnosis, 36-39

Defense mechanisms, for trauma, 60

Depression, after hypnosis, 50

Diet, effect on stress, 65-66

for wellness, 116-17, 139, 150-56

Digestion, importance to physical wellness, 156-57

Directing, of energy in self-hypnosis, 8

See also Visualization

Doctors, complications caused by, 95-96

Drugs, effect on stress, 65

E

Eating, effect on self-hypnosis, 30, 51

See also Diet

Egypt, use of hypnosis in, 19

Elevator deepening method, 37-38

Energy, of body, 101

universe constructed of, 100-101

Energy exchange process, to attain extra-ordinary state, 109-10

Environment, effect on health, 138-39

effect on self-hypnosis, 6-7, 30-31

Escalator deepening method, 38

Exercise, for stress reduction, 66

for wellness, 142, 158-60

Extra-ordinary states, of consciousness, 100-110

Eye fixation induction method, 33

F

Fats, in diet, 151-52

Fight-or-flight energy, 60

Fog, as transition plateau, 40

Food. *See* Diet
Food packaging, use of suggestion in, 13
Freud, Sigmund, hypnotism and, 23

G

Gestalt groups, 160-61
Ghost within the Machine. *See* Inner wisdom
Greece, use of hypnosis in, 19
Grounding process, to attain extra-ordinary state, 108-9
Growth, for high level wellness, 141-42

H

Habit, definition of, 73
  elements of, 74
Habit modification, by self-hypnosis, 4, 73-88
  techniques for, 84-86
Harmony with the earth process, for inner peace, 70
Headache, after hypnosis, 49
  tension, 63
Head roll induction method, 36
Healing, with self-hypnosis, 4, 53, 89-99
  techniques for, 97-98
Health. *See* High level wellness
High level wellness, 114-24
  physical dimension of, 149-60

psychological dimension of, 160-65
spiritual dimension of, 165-70
techniques for, 118-23, 170-76
Hiking, for wellness, 119
Holistic lifestyle, 136-48
Holistic philosophy, description of, 113
Homeostasis. *See* Inner wisdom
Hypertension, controlling by self-hypnosis, 4, 141
Hypnosis, self-. *See* Self-hypnosis
  use in primitive cultures, 19-20
  use as therapy, 20-24
Hypochondriacs, 95
Hysteria, treatment by hypnosis, 21

I

Induction methods, for self-hypnosis, 9-10, 32-36
Inner peace, techniques for, 69-71
Inner wisdom, 125-35
  process for, 132-34
Insomnia, self-hypnosis for, 30
Intuition. *See* Inner wisdom

J

Junk food. *See* Diet

K

Kirlian photography, 101

L

Leaving-and-returning deepening method, 38-39
Levitation, of hand, as induction method, 35
Liebeault, Jacque, hypnotism
and, 22

M

Magnetism, hypnotism and,
20-21
Maintenance, of health, 141
Mantra induction method, 35
Massage, for stress reduction,
157
Medical use of self-hypnosis,
53, 89-99
Meditation. *See* Self-hypnosis
Meditative walk process, for
high level wellness, 120
Mental energy, focusing of,
7-8
Mesmer, Franz, theory of
hypnotism, 20-21
Mind control. *See* Self-
hypnosis
Monotony induction tech-
nique, 34
Motivation, for self-hypnosis,
6
Muscle weakness induction
method, 35
Mystic, 101

N

Nausea, after hypnosis, 49
Nervous system, description
of, 60-61

Nutrition. *See* Diet

O

Oneness process, for inner
peace, 71

P

Packaging, food, use of sugges-
tion in, 13
Pain reduction, with self-
hypnosis, 53
Panic reaction, to self-
hypnosis, 52
Parasympathetic nervous
system, description of,
61
Parents, use of suggestion by,
14-15
Poisonous substance process,
of habit modification,
84-85
Position, for self-hypnosis, 30
Positive wellness. *See* High
level wellness
Posthypnotic suggestion. *See*
Suggestion
Power of suggestion. *See* Self-
hypnosis, Suggestion
Prayer, as induction method,
34
Precognition, 103-4
Preventive medicine, 141
Priority process, for self-
awareness, 144-45
Psychic, 101
Psychic phenomena. *See*
Extra-ordinary states

R

Relaxation, as ingredient of self-hypnosis, 6-7
program for, 62-67
self-hypnosis for, 29, 57-62
techniques of, 68-69
Religions, use of suggestion by, 13-14
Repetition, use in conditioning, 13
Rhythm patterns, of habits, 83
Ritual, in habit modification, 82
Rose process, to attain extra-ordinary state, 105-6
for inner peace, 70-71

S

Sadness, after hypnosis, 50
Saturated fats. See Fats
Self-hypnosis, coming out of, 41-42, 49
in daily life, 11-18
description of, 3-10, 42-46
development of, 24-25
environment for, 6-7, 30-31
frequency of, 31-32
hints for, 48-54
ingredients of, 6-8
stages of, 9-10, 32
techniques of, 29-47
timing of, 29-30, 51
Shell shock, treated by hypnosis, 24
Silva Mind Control, 25
Sleep, as stress relief, 63
Sleep partial, during day, 12

Sleep temples, in ancient Greece, 19
Spirit guide process, to attain extra-ordinary state, 106-8
Spontaneous remission, of disease, 5-6
Stage hypnotists, 23, 52-53
Staircase deepening method, 37
Stress, as cause of failure, 16
description of, 59
reduction of, 62-67
See also Relaxation
Stretching exercises. See Yoga
Sugar, 152
stress reduction and, 65
Suggestion, 16-18
in advertising, 12-13
by parents, 14-15
posthypnotic, 41, 48
language for, 96
in religion, 13-14
Sympathetic nervous system, description of, 60

T

Tai Chi, for stress reduction, 66
for wellness, 158-59
Tape recording. See Cassettes
Television commercials, suggestion in, 12-13, 135
Tension, as cause of illness, 15-16
headaches, 63
See also Stress
Total checkup process, for self-awareness, 143-44

Total Diet, for high level well-
    ness, 116-17, 142
Touching. *See* Massage
Transition plateau, 39-40
Trauma, description of, 59

                U

Upward gaze induction method,
    33

                V

Visualization, use in self-
    hypnosis, 8-9
  for habit modification, 79-80
  for healing, 90-91
  for relaxation, 68
Vital force. *See* Inner wisdom

                W

Water level process, for inner
    peace, 71
Weakest link process, for high
    level wellness, 118
Weight loss, Yoga and, 159
Wellness, *See* High level well-
    ness
Willpower, in breaking habits,
    75-76
Will to Die, definition of, 144
Will to Live, 128-29
  definition of, 5
Work, in holistic lifestyle, 136-37

                Y

Yoga, for stress reduction, 66
  for wellness, 119, 158-59